THE FORGOTTEN ARTS

*Yesterday's Skills
Adapted to Today's Materials*

Book Five

From

YANKEE® BOOKS

A division of Yankee Publishing Incorporated
Dublin, New Hampshire

Clarissa M. Silitch, Editor

John W. White, Designer

First Edition
Third Printing, 1986
Copyright 1982, by Yankee Publishing Incorporated
Printed in the United States of America.

Library of Congress Catalog Card No. 82-50198

ISBN: 0-911658-35-1

Contents

Weaving on a Tape Loom

by Miriam Dolloff Chesley

IN COLONIAL TIMES MOST HOUSEHOLDS MADE THEIR OWN house furnishings — rugs, curtains, bed covers, and linens — as well as the family's clothing from home-woven textiles. The tapes, cords, and fringes needed to bind, gather, fasten, hang, and, if time allowed, decorate these items were woven at home on a simple, handmade wooden heddle (Fig.1). These early tapes were woven from wool and linen threads spun on the family spinning wheel from carded wool and prepared flax, and they were usually the natural color of the fiber. Occasionally dyed threads were used in the warping of the loom.

Beautiful hand-woven tapes similar to those woven in Colonial times can be made today in the same easy way. When used in finishing and decorating household furnishings and clothes and accessories of either contemporary or Colonial design, they add a custom touch.

A considerable timesaver for the contemporary weaver is the availability of the necessary threads at the local yarn shop. The wide variety of colors, shades, and types of threads (such as embroidery floss and crochet cotton) makes the weaving of color-coordinated or matching tapes an exciting and rewarding companion craft to sewing, needlework, and knitting. Wherever possible, insist on colorfast thread or floss.

MAKING A TAPE LOOM

The main piece of equipment needed for weaving tapes is a handmade wooden heddle variously referred to as a tape loom, braid loom, gallus frame, knee loom, lap loom, or box loom, or by several other terms referring either to the woven product or the method by which the loom is supported. It is made by cutting a series of alternating holes and vertical slots into a thin board and then shaping the board so that it can be held firmly during the weaving process.

Almost any collection of American primitive antiques in a shop or historical museum will include a tape loom or two. A fascinating study can be made of their differences: some were artfully carved as a labor of love and others were hurriedly hacked as a matter of immediate necessity. But each one is unique according to the skill, imagination, and ingenuity of its maker.

Because of the many perforations and slots in the dry wood, antique looms are extremely fragile and should probably not be used for weaving. However, with a rough sketch and the approximate measurements of an original loom, a very useful reproduction can be made from a thin board, with an X-acto knife, a hand drill, and a coping saw, if available. My cousin, Ned Dolloff, and I have made and sold over 200 copies of the 1790 tape loom passed down in my husband's family. Relatively small, these looms are eminently portable, and still available should you prefer to purchase a loom rather than make your own. (Write us at the address given at the end of this chapter for details.)

To make a loom of your own design, obtain a thin board of clear

Fig. 1. Opposite page. *Author weaving on her homemade heddle, or loom.*

pine which is ⅜ inch thick, 5 or more inches wide, and at least 16 inches long. Such a board can be purchased at a building-supply store or a woodworking mill, where it can be planed to order from a thicker board. Remember that, in weaving, the loom is held upright between your knees, so do not choose too heavy a board.

On a piece of cardboard the same size as your board, draw the basic design of the loom by marking off inch squares and sketching in the locations of the 4 essential elements, i.e. the knee scoops and hanging hole in the handle and the holes and slots in the body (Fig. 2). Adjust the knee scoops to fit the weaver by cutting shallow scoops into the cardboard handle, trying the model out for size, and, if necessary, recutting the knee scoops to fit. Center the hanging hole in the handle. Draw the 2 outermost slots on the body ½ inch in from the sides, and then mark off as many slots as possible in between, bearing in mind that slots will be at least ¹/₁₆ inch wide and the thin slats left between should be at least ¼ inch wide. The holes will be drilled with a ¹/₁₆-inch bit in the geometrical center of each slat and at a comfortable weaving level. You may have to raise or lower the slots (minimum length 6 inches) once you have decided the best location for the holes. This is why making a cardboard model first is a good idea.

Some early looms were left rough and unadorned. However, most of the looms that were kept as heirlooms had been made more

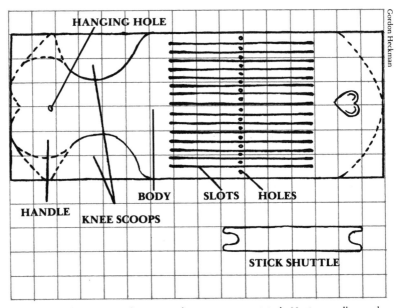

Fig. 2. *Basic loom pattern drawn to scale — 1 square = 1 inch. Netting needle may be used instead of stick shuttle.*

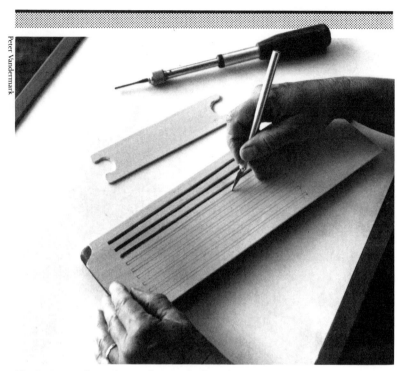

Fig. 3. *Cutting slots in loom with X-acto knife. Holes marked for drilling.*

decorative by shaping the outline and adding scratch-carved initials or dates, and simple designs (Fig. 2). The handle is uppermost when the loom is hung on the wall, and may easily be shaped into a disk, a heart, or a fan.

When you have completed your cardboard pattern, trace it onto the board and carve, drill, and saw it out as necessary (Fig. 3). Sand the loom and treat with a wood finish such as Minwax (plain or with a stain). When the loom has dried, wax with paste wax to keep it from drying and splitting. If, after all your labors, the loom should split, do not despair. Use wood glue, staples, wire, or small pieces of wood to repair and strengthen the weak spots, just as they did in Colonial times!

Additional Equipment. To complete your weaving setup you will need: (1) A shuttle for your weft thread. A 1x6-inch stick shuttle can be cut from a thin, flat stick (Fig. 3). A netting needle purchased in a weavers' shop or marine-supply store is even better, as it holds the weft threads more securely. (2) A flat stick of approximately 1x18 inches is required as a point of attachment for the warp threads. (3) A long belt or cord with a loop tied at both ends to secure the stick at your waist. As the tape is woven you will roll it up on the flat "waist stick" by turning the stick in the loops.

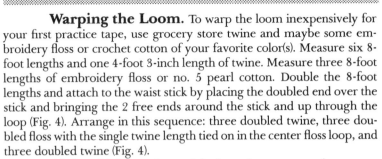

Warping the Loom. To warp the loom inexpensively for your first practice tape, use grocery store twine and maybe some embroidery floss or crochet cotton of your favorite color(s). Measure six 8-foot lengths and one 4-foot 3-inch length of twine. Measure three 8-foot lengths of embroidery floss or no. 5 pearl cotton. Double the 8-foot lengths and attach to the waist stick by placing the doubled end over the stick and bringing the 2 free ends around the stick and up through the loop (Fig. 4). Arrange in this sequence: three doubled twine, three doubled floss with the single twine length tied on in the center floss loop, and three doubled twine (Fig. 4).

With the stick in your lap and the loom between your knees, you will have both hands free to thread the warp ends through the heddle's holes and slots in sequence. Make sure that the warp threads will stretch in a straight line from the waist stick, through the loom, to the place where the knot is attached, by centering them in the heddle. This practice tape will use 19 spaces. Thread 5 twine ends, 2 floss ends, 1 twine, 1 floss, 1 twine, 2 floss ends, and 5 twine ends. Pull all the threads out straight and tie together in a knot at the farther end (Fig. 5).

Load your shuttle or netting needle with twine. Place the knotted warp threads over a doorknob, bedpost, or hook. Attach the stick at your waist by slipping one loop of your waist cord over an end, passing the cord around behind your back and putting the other loop over the other end of the stick. Sit in a comfortable straight chair (a desk chair on wheels

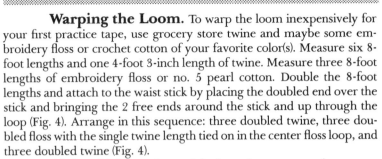

Peter Vandermark photos

Fig. 4. Left. *Attaching warp threads to waist stick. See inset for detail.*

Fig. 5. Above. *Knotted ends of warp are slipped over bedpost or other fixed object.*

is perfect) positioned a suitable distance from the attached knot of warp threads so that the threads are held fairly taut. Hold the heddle between your knees.

WEAVING THE TAPE

Start with the shuttle or netting needle in your right hand. Leave a foot of twine free for weaving. Begin to weave by pressing down on the warp threads with your left hand at a point halfway between the waist stick and the heddle. The threads in the slots will be pushed down below those that are permanently held in one position in the holes (Fig. 6). The space formed between the warp threads is called a "shed," and the weft material is passed through this space. To anchor the free weft end, pass it around the side warp thread and place it in the same shed. Pass the netting needle to the left hand and pull it tightly so that the tape becomes warp-faced (i.e., only the warp threads show). Now lift the warp threads with your right hand, and the threads in the slots will rise above those in the holes so that the second "shed" is formed. Before passing the weft back through, use the edge of the shuttle to "beat" the previous "shot" of weft material firmly into place. Now pass the shuttle through and to the right hand. The second "shot" has been made. Draw it taut, but not so much as to pull inward at the edges. Continue to lower the threads, beat, and make the shot; raise the threads, beat, and make the shot, keeping an even tension on both the warp and the weft threads. As the

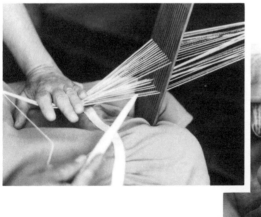

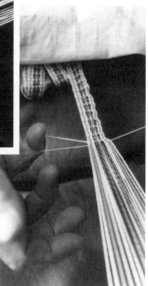

Fig. 6. Above. *Forming the "shed" between warp threads by pressing down on all the threads.*

Fig. 7. Right. *As woven tape exceeds comfortable reaching distance, it is rolled up on waist stick.*

tape begins to exceed your comfortable reach, roll it up on the stick and continue to weave (Fig. 7). When it is difficult to make another shed because so little warp thread length remains, wrap the weft thread around the tape and tie. Clip it. Untie the warp knot and draw the warp threads back through the loom and trim. Unroll the tape from the waist stick, slide the warp loops off the stick, tie, and trim.

The tape you have just made can be sewn onto clothing or household linens for a decorative touch. It is particularly attractive on unbleached muslin. Before sewing it on, shrink the tape by washing it the same way you will be laundering the article to be decorated. You may wish to test the tape for colorfastness by pressing it while still damp in a fold of white material such as an old sheet. If, in weaving, you insert the weft from the same side each time by passing the shuttle containing the weft under the warp threads between shots and changing the sheds as usual, you will produce a round woven cord that makes a perfect drawstring for the neck of a blouse, the waist of a skirt or slacks, or the bottom of a blouson.

Short pieces of tape make ideal hanging loops for washcloths, hand towels, pot holders, sweaters, and so on. Encourage your family to keep a tidy house by installing Shaker wall pegs in the kitchen, bath, and bedrooms. Then weave long lengths of tape to match your decor and install hanging loops on everything lying about on the furniture, counters and floor — except, of course, the dog and cat. Your subtle hint will not guarantee a neat home, but at least it's a beautiful try!

Once you have mastered the art of backstrap weaving with a fixed heddle, you will be able to produce an amazing variety of useful as well as decorative tapes, trims, straps, belts, and cords by paying careful attention to your choices from the following list of variables:

1) Size, texture, and color of warp and weft threads.
2) Number of warp threads used.
3) Arrangement of different colored warp threads in a pattern.
4) Force used in pulling the warp and beating the weft.

Any questions or comments on tape looms or this chapter will be happily answered by the author if sent to Box 416, North Scituate, MA 02060, accompanied by a self-addressed, stamped envelope.

Reseating Chairs with Cane and Rush

by Barbara Radcliffe Rogers

A CHAIR WITHOUT A SEAT IS NOT A VERY USEFUL THING. But to a Yankee, even a seatless chair is too good to throw away. In times past one could buy pressed-fiber seats to nail in place over the broken cane, but no longer. When the caning or rush has gone, there's nothing to do but hang the chair in the barn or take up the task of reseating it.

A chair with a series of little holes or a groove all around the seat rails is meant for caning. Perhaps the broken seat is still hanging there, in which case it is characterized by rows of interwoven cane forming tiny octagonal holes.

Reseating is not an impossible skill. On the contrary, it is easy to do and requires only time, good instructions, and the proper materials. No practice needed; you can begin on your best chair. Should you make a mistake, you will be able to correct it without any damage to the chair.

Regardless of whether your chair requires reseating with cane or with rush, whatever other work may need to be done on the chair itself should be done first: gluing, refinishing, stenciling, or false graining should all be completed before reseating begins.

CANING

If you have the old cane, simply buy the same size; but if no caning remains, measure both the diameter of the holes around the seat and the distance between them. Purchase cane to fit as follows:

Superfine if holes are ⅛ inch and ⅜ inch apart
Fine fine if holes are ³/₁₆ inch and ½ inch apart
Fine if holes are ³/₁₆ inch and ⅝ inch apart
Medium if holes are ¼ inch and ¾ inch apart
Common if holes are ⁵/₁₆ inch and ⅞ inch apart

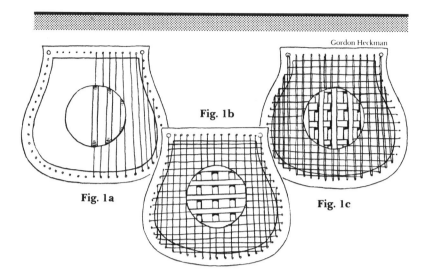

Gordon Heckman

Fig. 1b

Fig. 1a

Fig. 1c

Fig. 1. *Consecutive steps in cane weaving pattern (a, b, c, d). If chair front is wider than back, use side holes to complete first set of strands.*

It takes 250 feet of cane to do an average-size seat. Enough binder cane to go all around the edge is normally included when you purchase the seat cane. It is a little wider, and should be removed from the roll of weaving cane so it doesn't get used for weaving by mistake.

There is a plastic cane on the market, but you should not use this on old chairs because it looks like what it is — plastic. The cost of real cane is low, and it is better to use the right materials.

In the event that your chair doesn't have a series of holes around the seat, it will have a small groove around the edges of the opening. This type of chair uses cane webbing, which is a sheet of already woven cane. The webbing is cut to size, pressed into place, and secured with a strip of spline. This method is discussed later.

In addition to the cane, you will need a small bowl of warm water, some clip clothespins, 24 wooden pegs (which you can buy where you purchase your cane, whittle yourself, or which can be uncolored golf tees), glycerine, a sharp knife, a small cloth, and a pointed tool such as an ice pick or knitting needle.

Be sure all pieces of old seat are removed and that the holes are clear. Take one strand of cane from the bundle and roll it in a coil about 4 inches in diameter. Clip with a clothespin so that the cane will stay coiled. Put 1½ tablespoons of glycerine and a cup of warm water in the bowl, and soak the coiled cane in it for 20 minutes.

The most common procedure is to weave first from back to front, then from side to side, repeat each direction and then weave the 2 diagonals. Count the holes across the back. Put a peg in the center hole, or peg the 2 center holes if there is an even number. Repeat on the front.

Remove the cane from the water and replace it with another coil.

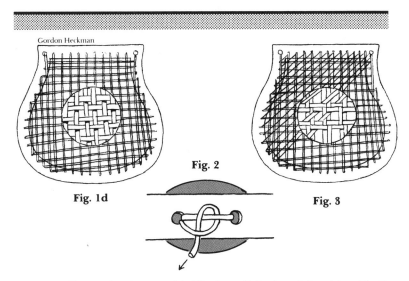

Fig. 2. *Tie off cane ends on bottom with half-hitches, pulled tight and clipped short.* **Fig. 3.** *Weaving pattern for first set of diagonal strands.*

Wipe excess water from cane and unclip it. Pull out the center back peg (or the right-hand one, if there are two) and push 5 inches of cane into the hole. Replace the peg, making sure that the cane is smooth side up. Remove the front center peg (or the right one, if there are two) and push a length of cane through from top. Be sure the cane isn't twisted, and peg it in place. *It should not be pulled tight,* — the slack will be taken up with the weaving. Continuing with the same piece of cane and moving to the right, bring the cane up through the next hole, be sure it is right side up, and stretch it to the back of the chair, parallel to the first strand. Continue back and forth until you reach the back corner. When it is apparent that the cane will not reach the other side, begin a new piece and end the old by placing a peg in that hole.

Do not use the corner hole unless it is larger than the others. In some chairs, the corner holes are enlarged to accommodate the extra strands of the diagonal weaving, in which case you may use them. Otherwise, go on to the first hole down the side and leave the corner empty for the time being.

Since the front edge of the chair is almost always wider than the back, you will have to use some of the side holes to complete the first set of strands. Your eye will tell you which hole to use in order to keep the cane parallel (Fig. 1). Do not carry the cane under the rail and inadvertently cover holes you will need later. Use separate shorter lengths of cane for these shorter edge lengths and secure their ends with pegs. Peg the last hole to keep cane in place and leave rest of cane attached. (If there is a lot, coil and secure with a clothespin to keep it out of way.) Weave the other half the same way.

Starting at the back-right side rail, in the hole next to the corner, peg the end in place and lay another set of strands from side to side right over the first back-to-front set (Fig. 1b). If the chair front is curved, use separate strands as you did on the sides.

Beginning again at the back center, repeat the first set of canes from back to front, laying these on top of the side-to-side set and using the same holes you used for the first set (Fig. 1c). Put the cane through the holes a little bit to the right of the first set if you can. This makes them lie parallel instead of directly atop one another and makes weaving easier later on.

When you have completed these three steps and have two sets back to front and one side to side, turn the chair over and fasten the loose ends by twisting them in half hitches around the cane that shows on the bottom (Fig. 2). Cut the ends, leaving ½ inch. If the cane has dried, you may need to dampen it with a cloth soaked in the water-glycerine solution.

Now you are ready to begin the weaving. Starting as you did before, on the right rail in the hole next to the back corner, lay a second series of side-to-side canes, this time weaving the cane *over* the top back-to-front strands and *under* the bottom ones (Fig. 1d).

A definite pattern of double weaving will emerge. If you have been completely lost until this point, you should begin to take hope here. The canes will draw together in pairs.

I find it easier to weave a few stitches with the end of the cane, then pull it all through and repeat this at intervals. Some people weave half the row with a short length and then pull it through, but I find it more manageable in shorter sections. To keep the tension even, peg the end of each row until you have woven the next. You should still not be pulling the cane tight.

When this fourth step is completed, tie off the ends (Fig. 2), using a single half hitch pulled tight. Trim ends. Using 2 pegs, push the canes together into close pairs, forming definite holes between each set. These

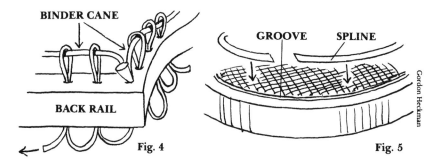

Fig. 4. *Application of binder cane.* **Fig. 5.** *Ready-woven webbing is attached to chair by wedging spline over it into groove in frame.*

even holes will make the final weaving easier.

Beginning at the back corner hole on the right, peg down a strand and head it toward the left front. Weave diagonally so the cane crosses *over* the front-to-back pairs and *under* the side-to-side pairs (Fig. 3). This is easiest if you run a piece of string or thread from corner to corner just to get you started in the right direction. Once started, you will follow a sequence straight to a hole in the opposite corner.

Weave with one hand on top and one under, pulling the cane through every few stitches. Don't pull at a sharp angle or the cane may break. When you complete the first strand, move toward the back and do each row in the same way, over the front-to-back and under the side-to-side pairs. You will have to double up on the holes every so often — just take the cane to the nearest hole in line with its path. You may also have to skip holes to keep the rows straight. The cane will pretty well tell you where it is going; as it reaches the rail it simply goes in the hole most directly in its path.

Repeat, beginning at the center, to complete the front right half of the seat. Tie off and trim cane ends as you go.

The final strands of the seat are woven diagonally in the opposite direction. Begin at the back corner hole on the left and go toward the front right. Weave *under* the front-to-back pairs and *over* the side-to-side pairs. Weave the front first, using holes that match the ones used on the other side. Use the holes you skipped before twice, so it will be even. Again, be careful not to carry the cane across holes on the bottom. Cut and tie the cane if necessary to avoid this.

Your chair will now look like a chair again and needs only the finishing touch of binder cane. If the seat is round, use one piece of binder all around. If it is square or the corners sharp, use a separate piece for each side. Very often the sides and front can use one long piece and the back a single short one.

Soak both the binder and a weaving cane in the water and glycerine as before. The weaving cane should be particularly pliable.

Lay the binder over the row of holes, putting one end of it through the corner hole and pegging it down. Beginning at this pegged end pull the weaving cane up through the hole, over the binder and back down through the same hole. On the underneath, move to the next hole and repeat. The binder lies along the top, held down by the series of loops along it (Fig. 4). If the holes are full, you may have to force an opening through with an ice pick. Tie off ends, and your chair is ready.

In the event that your chair has grooves instead of holes, obtain a piece of cane webbing 2 inches larger in each direction than the inside measurement of the chair seat and a piece of spline 2 inches longer than the chair's circumference. The tools you will need are a chisel (or large screwdriver), a sharp knife, a mallet, 5 wooden wedges (made especially for this and available wherever you buy the cane) and white glue. Soak the webbing and spline in warm water 30 minutes. Remove all the old webbing, glue, and spline from the chair, taking care not to damage the groove. Stubborn glue can often be removed with warm vinegar.

Place the wetted webbing on the chair and anchor it at intervals with 4 wedges. Using the mallet and fifth wedge, make a dent in the webbing all around the groove in the edge of the seat. This gives you an exact measurement line. With the webbing still in place, cut on a line ½ inch outside this groove line. Push the ½ inch of remaining webbing down into the groove, using the screwdriver or chisel. With a sharp knife, carefully cut off any that won't fit into the groove to keep any raw edges from sticking out.

Measure the soaked spline by pressing it lightly into the groove and miter-cut the ends so they fit together perfectly (Fig. 5). Remove spline and put a moderate amount of glue into the groove. Force the spline into the groove around the seat, pounding it with the mallet. Be sure it is in evenly. If any glue seeps out, remove it quickly with a damp cloth. Let the chair dry a day or so before sitting in it.

RUSH SEATS

Compared to caning a chair, fashioning rush seats is child's play! Rush may be used on any chair with a square or trapezoid seat frame made of 4 bars.

Chairs that were originally seated in woven splint like a basket

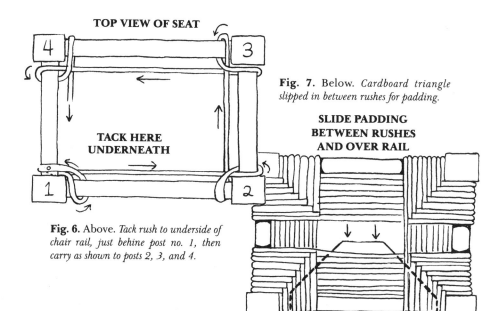

TOP VIEW OF SEAT

TACK HERE UNDERNEATH

Fig. 7. Below. *Cardboard triangle slipped in between rushes for padding.*

SLIDE PADDING BETWEEN RUSHES AND OVER RAIL

Fig. 6. Above. *Tack rush to underside of chair rail, just behine post no. 1, then carry as shown to posts 2, 3, and 4.*

Gordon Heckman

may be rewoven in rush — a far simpler process. As in caning, remove all old seating and refinish the chairs, if necessary, before beginning.

Real rush is a bit more difficult to deal with than its fiber substitutes because it does not keep a twist. You must twist it evenly and firmly as you work. You must also keep adding new pieces as you weave, which makes the work even more difficult. For these reasons, one of the substitutes is usually recommended for beginners.

A material called Fibrerush — a twisted cord made of paper — keeps its twist, comes in a continuous piece, and is difficult to tell from the real thing if properly used. It also wears well. Hong Kong grass is a real grass twisted by hand, hence slightly uneven, resembling real rush's uneven quality. It is more difficult to work than Fibrerush, but easier than the real thing because it is in a continuous roll.

Which should you use? If you are reseating an antique chair, real rush is historically correct, but trickier to handle. Fibrerush is just as serviceable, looks fine, and is much easier to work with, needing neither soaking nor twisting. As for strength and durability, it's a draw.

If you decide on Fibrerush, in the directions that follow simply ignore any directions for soaking, inserting new rushes, or twisting. Treat Hong Kong grass just like fiber, but soak it for 5 minutes first.

Rush must be soaked for 4 to 6 hours in warm water. When it is pliable and you can twist it without cracking or splitting it, wrap it in an

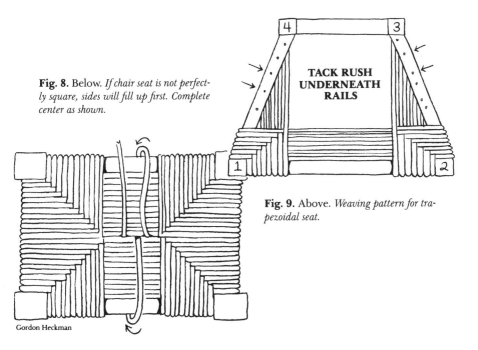

Fig. 8. Below. *If chair seat is not perfectly square, sides will fill up first. Complete center as shown.*

TACK RUSH UNDERNEATH RAILS

Fig. 9. Above. *Weaving pattern for trapezoidal seat.*

Gordon Heckman

old sheet to hold moisture. Before you use each piece, press it thoroughly by pulling it between your fingers to remove excess water. Cut off the thick bases if they have not already been removed.

The thickness of the rush is determined by the number of strands, but 3 is the usual number. It is difficult to twist in new pieces if fewer are used, and more make a bulky seat. Tie the rushes together at one end and practice twisting them before you begin. If necessary, cut them to different lengths so you won't be adding new pieces all in one spot. The two continuing rushes strengthen the spot where you've twisted in a new piece.

Just to make directions easier, number the corner posts on the top side of the chair 1, 2, 3, and 4, beginning at the front left and going to the front right, back right, and back left. Tack the end of the rush to the underside of the rail, just behind post no. 1 (Fig. 6). If you are using continuous coil, cut off about 25 to 30 feet and re-coil it to make it easier to handle.

Twist the cord evenly and firmly and bring over the top of the front rail, then under it, and cross over it from right to left and bring out over the left rail. Continue under that rail and across the front of the chair, parallel to the front rail, over the right rail, under it, then over the rush and front rail, as close to post no. 2 as you can, under the front rail and on to the back at post no. 3 (Fig. 6).

Repeat, going over and under the back rail, over and under the right rail, and across to post no. 4 (Fig. 6). Continue this same weave, keeping the rush stretched firmly and twisted evenly. Treat the already-in-place strands as though they were part of the rail. Traditionally the rush is not twisted on the bottom, but there is no reason why it can't be.

If you are adding rushes and do not twist on the underside, all your additions will have to be made on the top or sides in order to hold in the twist.

Be sure the corners are wrapped in exactly the same way, and are perfectly even. If you wrap one incorrectly it will show up as glaringly as a misspelling of your own name, so fix it immediately.

It is a good idea to pad the seat slightly to prevent the edges of the rails from breaking through the rush. On old chairs, odd ends of rush were forced through from underneath to pad the edges of the rail. A more modern (although certainly not new!) method is to cut triangles of corrugated cardboard from a carton. Cut the points off as shown and slip cardboard between the rushes on top of the rails after 2 or 3 inches of weaving (Fig. 7). Continue to weave right over the cardboard.

If the chair seat is not a perfect square, the sides will fill up before the front is done. In this case, fill in the center by bringing the rush up through the rushes between the two center strands, over the back rail, under the back half of the strands, up between the 2 center ones (where you came up before in the other direction) over and under the front rail, and back and forth until you have filled in the entire center (Fig. 8). When you are finished, take the rush down through the center, separate the three strands, and tie each in a square knot around the nearest span of rush on the bottom. With Fibrerush, simply tie to a convenient span using a square knot.

Should the front rail be longer than the back, as in a trapezoidal seat, you must weave a few strands on the front and side rails only until a square is formed. Begin 2 or 3 inches back on the left rail and tack the end of the rush to its underside. Bring it straight to the front rail, next to post no. 1, over and under it, over and under the left rail, and across the front — just as you would for a square chair. But when you complete corner no. 2 and head back toward the back rail, stop and tack the rush to the right rail at the same distance from the front rail as you began on the left (Fig. 9).

Do this again, moving the beginning and end of each rush back up the side rails until you reach the back and a square is formed. Then continue as for a square seat.

When the seat is completed, let it dry thoroughly, then treat with 3 coats of clear shellac, letting each coat dry before applying the next.

SUPPLIES

A good selection of cane and rush, as well as pegs, wedges, webbing, spline, and other supplies, is available by mail from New Hampshire Cane and Reed Co. on Daniel Webster Highway in Suncook, New Hampshire. The mailing address is Box 176, Suncook, NH 03275.

You can gather and prepare your own rushes without much trouble if you have a stand of flag or cattails available. Cut them when they are full grown and the very tips are just beginning to brown. Cut off the thick base portion.

Tie them in loose bunches and hang them in a dark, dry place (the attic or shed loft is perfect) for a few weeks to dry. They are ready to use when almost crisp, with no feeling of moisture at all.

How to Care for Quilts, Old and New

Deborah Karr

by Bets Ramsey

*"I have an old quilt I'd like you to see.
It's silk and velvet, all covered with the most beautiful
stitches imaginable."*

*"My mother left me half a dozen quilt tops
and I've never done anything to finish them."*

*"I found an old scrap of a quilt in a junk shop and paid 50¢ for it.
It could use some mending, though."*

*"My beautiful old white stuffed quilt is turning brown.
What can I do?"*

I ONCE FOUND A MUDDY OLD PICKLE DISH QUILT IN A PILE OF rags behind a junk shop. The quilt-back, which had caught my eye, was a nineteenth-century brown and red engraved-print material, and the top was home-dyed brown and red muslin. "You can have it for a dollar," the dealer said. It was wet and full of mildew and roly-bugs, but I wanted to save that quilt. I paid my dollar, gingerly shook out the bugs, and dropped the quilt in the trunk of the car. At home, I dumped it in a galvanized tub in the backyard and turned on the garden hose. When some of the mud was washed away, I added mild detergent and worked with a plumber's helper to loosen more of the dirt. After much plunging and several rinsings, the quilt was dried on the clothesline. Only then was it fit to bring in the house, and, in spite of harsh treatment, it was quite presentable. Its condition determined the manner in which it was washed.

A very old quilt must be given kind treatment if it is to be washed. First, determine colorfastness. To do this, fill a medicine dropper with a diluted washing agent, wet a small area, and blot dry. If any color comes out on the blotter, the colors are not fast and you will probably choose not to wash the quilt. If all seems safe, proceed.

When a quilt is heavy with water, the filler swells, and old, rotted threads will give way. Therefore, it is necessary to minimize the strain. One way of doing this is to make 2 sheets the size of the quilt by seaming together inexpensive nylon net. Place the quilt between the net pieces and baste together. The net will provide extra strength during the washing process. In order to cut down on handling, do the washing in a bathtub.

Place the quilt in the tub and let water of moderate temperature run to cover it. A gentle water softener added to clear water will loosen accumulation of surface dirt. A bath sponge, used gently, will help in working the soap or detergent through the fabric in the second bath. A number of rinsings will be required to remove all the soap. During and between rinsings the quilt has remained in the tub in order to subject its old stitches to a minimum of strain. During the final stage of squeezing out the water, some assistance may be needed as the quilt will be very heavy. After draining, squeeze as much water as possible from the quilt while it still rests in the tub. Gradually lift it and, with help, press the water out between flattened hands. Do not twist or wring dry or stitches will pop. Blotting may be done with large bath towels. Finally, hang the quilt outdoors to dry, preferably in the shade on a day when there is a breeze. Pin parallel edges of the quilt to 2 clotheslines to distribute the weight and further reduce strain, or lay the quilt out flat on towels.

If the quilt is in good condition and has been tested for colorfastness, you may choose instead to wash it in a heavy-duty washing machine, using a mild cleanser. It is important to get all the soap out. You cannot rinse it too much. Hang as described above. When the quilt is dry, do not attempt to iron it; you will only be ironing *in* wrinkles.

For the old and valuable quilt, home cleaning is not recommended. A museum curator may be able to direct you to a place that specializes in antique-fabric restoration.

The Division of Textiles of the Smithsonian Institution has developed certain methods for caring for its cotton and linen textiles. After testing for colorfastness, a quilt is supported throughout the entire process of cleaning by placing it on a large sheet of fiber-glass screening and covering it with the same material. With the quilt between the 2 screens, a low-power, hand vacuum cleaner is run over the surface to remove dirt and dust. If the color is not fast, vacuuming will be the sole method of cleaning used.

When a quilt is to be washed the laboratory's way, it is done in a basin large enough to hold the quilt without folding it. Such a basin can be made from 4 boards joined to make a rectangular frame, with a large plastic sheet stretched across it loosely enough to make a shallow basin within the framework. With the open-basin method, the quilt can be placed on the screen and lowered into it, with no hand-lifting necessary during the entire operation.

The research chemist advocates a nonionic detergent as the cleaning agent and water at about 90°F. Distilled water is used at the laboratory in order to eliminate any residue of minerals or impurities. Soft water is next best; hard water is to be avoided.

In the laboratory, the first step in washing a quilt is to soak it in the washing solution for an hour, then raise the screen and let the dirty water drain. The quilt may be gently hosed. If the first water is yellow or dirty, the procedure is repeated 1 or more times. When the quilt appears clean, it is rinsed several times and hosed between rinsings. "Never scrub, beat, or squeeze an antique quilt," says the lab's director, Maureen Collins McHugh. After the final rinsing, the quilt remains on the screen to drain and dry.

McHugh explained the museum's basic philosophy about textile cleaning. Commercial cleaners want to make fabrics *look* clean, whereas the museum wants to *preserve* them. Surprisingly enough, the Smithsonian did not begin to do its own cleaning until the textile department moved to the new Museum of History and Technology, in 1963.

The technician is interested in returning the cotton or linen to its natural, or neutral, state by removing acid and particles that cause abrasion and wear. If the appearance of the textile is improved in the process, so much the better, but it is not the primary concern.

Generally speaking, quilt making was a practical art until the era of the Victorian crazy quilt. Fabrics in the Victorian masterpiece crazy quilt, instead of being simple and practical, are usually silks, satins, brocades, velvets, wools, and novelties. Very likely, the "quilt" is unquilted. The crazy quilt's tour de force is the amazing array of stitches that join and decorate the pieces — mementos and keepsakes of sentimental value. The crazy quilt was made for show, and never intended for practical use or laundering. Now the fragile old silk and satin is usually too weak to withstand dry cleaning. Nevertheless, because of its very impracticality, this type of quilt can often be found in good condition.

Occasionally one finds a quilt with wool fleece or a woolen blanket as filler. Proper precautions must be taken in washing it. Use cool water and an agent such as Woolite, made for washing wool. Wash quickly, and dry away from heat. If you are uncertain what the filler is, rip a seam a short distance and examine the inside. Fiber tests can help determine the contents. A sample of cotton burns quickly, smells like burning paper, and leaves a small gray ash. Wool burns slowly, goes out easily, and smells like burning hair. Synthetics melt like cotton candy.

I once saw an old pieced brown and white quilt that had a worn woolen blanket as filler. The brown calico was softly faded, like an old photograph. A bargain-hunter found it in a secondhand shop. Determined to wash away years of grime, she gave it the usual laundry treatment, lots of hot soapy water, and, of course, the wool shrank. The quilt is a total loss unless its owner has the patience to take out the stitches of the quilting, bit by bit, and requilt the top.

Quilts, whether they are used often or not, can be kept fresh and unspotted by periodically hanging them outdoors for sun and air. When storing them again, fold them differently each time to avoid creases that cause the fibers to break. Old towels or undyed sheets, loosely wrapped, make the best covering and will prevent any direct contact with wood, which is acidic and damaging to cotton and linen. Paper and tissue paper, being made of wood, have the same acidic property and are not suitable wrapping for the same reason. Quilts may be placed in closets, chests of drawers, wardrobes, or cedar chests, and should be in an area of relatively even humidity and cool temperature. Avoid cardboard boxes, which have a tendency to become damp in rainy weather. A quilt may be aired just by using it on a bed, and why not?

It is a chore to look after quilts if one never takes time to enjoy them. There are many ways to use quilts: as a quilt, as a spread, as a throw on the foot of the bed, or just hung over a blanket rack to please the eye. Quilts may be hung as room dividers or wall panels. Salvage good portions of ragged quilts for pillows and small hangings.

My remarks have been directed primarily toward the care of old quilts. New ones do not present the same problems. Synthetic fillers are washable, and almost all colors are permanently set. Apply the same principles of airing, storing, and cleaning in caring for them, and do not expose the fabrics to direct sunlight. Not only will they fade, but light will weaken fibers and cause rot.

"A stitch in time saves nine" is one of those adages we usually learn the hard way. It is much easier to mend a quilt with a few broken seams than it is a tattered one. See that little tears are mended promptly.

On some quilts, one fabric may give way before the rest of the body. This is especially true of print fabrics that were made with an early commercial brown dye. Rather than trying to impose new material onto old, stitch a piece of fine net or illusion over the worn spot. This will cover the worn place and hold the deteriorating material together but will not change the character of the quilt, as a patch of modern material would. The Smithsonian's textile department uses silk organza: the silk overlay pieces are sewn on with ravelings of the same cloth.

It is surprisingly difficult to find mending pieces that are appropriate matches with period fabrics. Unless you are very clever, the contemporary patch you put on a quilt made in 1942 will be quite obvious. It is possible to find likely mending pieces at rummage sales and thrift shops in garments that have aged, as the quilts have done. Reproduction calico and other prints are available to simulate old patches and therefore reduce contrast. To minimize the newness, wash, bleach, and sun them first. As a general rule it is advisable to work within the time and style framework of the quilt's period when making repairs.

Unfinished tops are in abundance. What can be done about them? If you have never quilted, join a class at the local YWCA, museum, or church. Learn the fundamentals of quilting and organize a quilting bee. If you are reluctant to do your own quilting, the local government extension service may be able to furnish names of quilting groups. The Stearns & Foster Co., Wyoming & Williams, Cincinnati, OH 45215, manufacturers of quilt filler, maintains a list of quilters. Cost and quality vary, but you can ask to see a sample of quilting and get a price estimate before contracting for a job. Or, write quilting groups advertising in the following publications: *Quilter's Newsletter,* Leman Publications, Box 394, Wheatridge, CO 80033; National Quilting Association's *Newsletter,* P.O. Box 62, Greenbelt, MD 20770; *Farmers & Consumers Market Bulletin,* Georgia Department of Agriculture, 19 Hunter St., S.W., Atlanta, GA 30334; and *Progressive Farmer,* Shades Creek Parkway, Birmingham, AL 35209.

Laying a Slate Roof

by Edie Clark

I N COLOR, TEXTURE, STRENGTH, AND DURABILITY, NO other roofing material can compete with slate. A good slate roof will last a lifetime. To bear testimony to that, there are plenty of old houses with 80-year-old slate roofs still as good as new. However, the cost of both labor and materials generally runs to about $300 per "square" (i.e., 100 square feet of slate roofing), a high price even for several lifetimes.

To bring the price within reach, we decided to lay our own slate roof. The labor is not so much expertise as it is muscle work. By combing the want ads of the local newspapers daily, we found more than enough used slate available, in the more reasonable price range of 50¢ a slate (new ones, depending on the size, run roughly $1.50 to $2 apiece). Thus, we thought we were all set when we'd bought the necessary 13 squares of slate that had been carefully removed from an old barn in Griswold-ville, Massachusetts, and got the bonus of a brief course in slating from the kind man who sold them to us. But our confidence lagged when we faced the awesome job of getting the more than 4 tons (8,400 pounds) of slate up onto the roof of our new house. (Slate loses a bit of its weight with age: standard [³/₁₆ to ¼ inch] *new* slate weighs 850 pounds per square; ours, new, would have weighed 11,050 pounds). So, while we cast about for someone to lead us through the slate-laying process, we roofed the house with inexpensive roll roofing, which kept us dry a good 3 years. Meanwhile, we stored the slate in a dry barn, upright, as advised, rather than flat. Eventually, we did find a guide: Paul Bolton, a carpenter who has worked on slate roofs for 13 years. Four of us, two completely inexperienced, one with general roofing experience, and Paul, sailed smoothly through the job, in spite of the hot and muggy 95°F. July weather, in three 8-hour days.

I should emphasize here that without being properly acquainted with the rudiments of roofing, including especially valleys and flashing, you shouldn't attempt to lay slate. Outlined here are the peculiarities of *slate* roofing; simple roofing techniques are implied. For more in-depth information, there's an invaluable book, recently reproduced by, and available directly from, Vermont Structural Slate Company, Fair Haven, VT 05743. This 84-page manual, *Slate Roofs,* was originally published in 1926 by the now defunct National Slate Association; it now has the reputation of being the slater's bible and will undoubtedly tell you more than you need to know about slate.

If you decide to use new rather than used slate, you'll find that new roofing slate is hard, yet not impossible, to find. It's often more convenient to deal directly with a quarry rather than ordering through a local roofing company. There are several quarries listed at the end of this chapter that can process your order.

Slates come in varying sizes, ranging all the way from 12x6 inches, which requires 533 pieces per square, to the hefty size of 24x16 inches, which requires only 86 pieces per square. Thus, if you order slates for repair, you would pay by the piece; but ordering by the square stabilizes the price of a square at between $180 and $220, regardless of the size of the pieces. Though a combination of large and small slates can undoubtedly give a distinctive texture to a roof, medium slates are easier to handle than large, and require less nailing than small slates.

Be sure to sort through used slates carefully, discarding any that are cracked or appear too worn. To test a questionable slate, set it on its end lengthwise and lean into it with the heel of your hand; if it's not up to another 100 years of roofing, it will snap. Another test: hold the slate lightly between your finger and thumb and tap it gently. A sound slate will ring like a china cup.

Good slating tools are essential. There are 3 tools that make the job a lot easier: a slater's hammer, a ripper, and a stake (Fig. 1). A slate cutter, which works rather like a paper cutter, is useful too. The hammer is an invaluable and economical tool used for 3 important functions: cutting, punching, and nailing the slate. The stake provides a straight cutting edge and, although useful, can be substituted with almost anything, including the edge of the scaffold or the tailgate of a pickup. The ripper is used primarily for repair; although you may not need to use it on the initial job, sometime in the future you will need one. All three of these are still available new, though many slaters insist that the tools made now don't hold a candle to the older tools, stronger because they were forged from a higher-quality steel. Old ones can be found only by careful searching through antique-tool shops, flea markets, and auctions. New tools can be purchased from John Stortz and Son, Inc., 210 Vine Street, Philadelphia, PA 19106. Stortz has been making these tools for some 75 years, and each tool is forged from steel in one piece. The Vermont Structural Slate Company, mentioned earlier, will send you a list of sources for buying slaters' tools.

Preliminaries taken care of, it's time to tackle the roof. At this point, as you look from ground to roof and back again, contemplating tonnage and the strength of your back, the sight of those great stacks of slate makes the high commercial cost of laying a slate roof completely understandable. Some roofers won't do it at all. A strip-shingle roof suddenly looks very attractive. After all, an 80-pound bundle of asphalt shingles can be hefted onto the roof on your shoulder, and with 3 bundles per square, you'll be roofed up tight long before you will with the slate.

Slating is not a job for a faint heart or a weak back, but there are ways to make the job go faster. To cut down on ladder work, erect staging (which can be rented quite reasonably) full length across the house, flush with the eaves. Ladders can then lean directly on the roof, and the slate can be stockpiled on the staging, handy to the job. Cover any windows near the staging or scaffold with plywood; the slate is heavy and sharp and really flies once you get going.

Gordon Heckman

Fig. 1. *Slating tools, clockwise from top: ripper, hammer, stake.*

Keep the stake handy. Some slaters drive the stake, which has a pointed tail for the purpose, into a board on the lower scaffold; some move it with them along the roof. There's always a piece of slate that needs fitting so the stake or a suitable substitute should be ready to hand for cutting, trimming, or punching the slate.

The most delicate part of laying slate is the nailing. The copper nails used by slaters of the past are still available, but very expensive. Cheaper, but regrettably not as good for the purpose, are galvanized roofing nails. Whichever type of nail you use, calculate the nail length necessary as you would for any other type of roofing: the thickness of the slate x 2 plus 1 inch = nail length needed. The slates laid on the roof actually hang from the nails. Used slate will already have holes, but possibly in the wrong places. The nail holes, always 2 (or 4 for slates over 20 inches long) should be 1¼ to 2 inches from each edge and ¼ to ⅓ the length of the slate from the top. Thus, if your slates are 12 inches long, the hole should be punched 3 to 4 inches from the top of the slate.

Holes are punched in the slate with a single, sharp blow of the pointed end of the slater's hammer, through the *backside* of the slate. This punches the backside clean and shatters the area around the hole on the upright side, making a nest (countersink) for the nail so it will rest free of the slate on top of it. The nail should sit in the hole so the head just touches the slate. This is the catch-22 of slating: if driven in too far — "homed" — the nail will break through the slate and won't hold it; if not driven in far enough, the nail head will break through the slate that covers it from the course above. Or at the very least it will tip the slate up, making it easy for the slate to be lifted and broken off by high winds.

Nailing slate is a precise skill, the only "skill" required in slate roofing — the rest is thinking, planning, and lifting. It is well worthwhile to practice nailing with odd pieces before starting to lay the actual roof. When you're done, the nail head should be below the *surface* of the slate, not tight to the slate, and the whole slate should be free to move slightly. Each slate has to be nailed properly. If you aren't satisfied that it is sitting right, rip it out and do it over, even at the sacrifice of the slate. After all, it's *permanence* that you're after, and poorly laid slate will only cause trouble later.

Likewise, practice cutting and punching slate before you begin the roof. Even at used prices slate is an expensive item, but sacrificing a few for practice initially can give you a greater facility for making accurate cuts way up into the fifteenth course.

To cut, measure for your cut and scribe a line on the back side of the slate. With the pointed end of the slater's hammer, punch a tight row of holes straight on that line and break it clean along that row. Rest the good piece on your stake or other flat-edged surface and hang the ragged punched line just over the edge. With the shear edge of the shank of the hammer, shave the line to a straight edge. If you have a slate cutter, the procedure is more or less the same, but somewhat easier.

Figure the "exposure" of your slate by deducting 3 inches from the length of the slate you're using and dividing that by 2. For example, if your slates are 18 inches long, subtract 3 and divide the result, 15, by 2. Thus, each slate should have 7½ inches exposed to the weather. Make certain that all your slates are the same size. If they are, you can proceed using one flat figure for exposure. If not, you'll have to recalculate when the size changes. A very popular and attractive roof used to be the graduated roof which had the smallest and thinnest slates at the peak of the roof, widening to larger and thicker ones at the eaves. If you've bought an odd-size lot of slates, sort them and graduate them in the most attractive way possible, always remembering to adjust the exposure as the size changes. Slates of distinctive color or size can also be used to make a pattern in your roof, if you're bold enough to try it. Even a single band of a contrasting color such as red or purple across the top or middle can add distinction without much extra effort.

Begin slating by nailing a ⅜-inch clapboard along the edge of the roof, flush with the eaves. This raises the bottom row of slates subtly, just enough so that each successive course will lay flat. Then run a row of slates *lengthwise,* flush with the bottom of the clapboard. That's your starter slate, and you're ready to begin ascending just as you would with regular shingles.

Finish the ridge with a copper strip as wide as the exposure of your slate, using copper nails. Slate *can* be used to seal the ridge, but this is fancy, and complicated, and not very common even among the older roofs. Complete instructions for either method are given in the book *Slate Roofs,* mentioned earlier.

Laying slate is hard and precise work. The cutting and fitting can be frustrating and the progress slow at times, especially compared with what could be considered the breezy progress of roofing with asphalt shingles. If possible, don't choose the hot July weather we worked in. Cool spring or autumn weather should be ideal.

There's nothing like your own slate roof to make you more aware of the inordinate beauty of slate. Weather conditions cause kaleidoscopic changes: sun and rain subtly alter the colors; strong, early-morning sunlight lends a miraculous, 3-dimensional quality; the silver glint of moonlight on the roof is nearly magical. And there's nothing like the sound of fresh-fallen snow sliding off the slate roof like thunder, sending cats scattering in all directions.

SOURCES.

Cut Slate, Inc., Depot Street, Fair Haven, VT 05743
Rising and Nelson Slate Company, West Pawlet, VT 05775
Vermont Structural Slate Company, Fair Haven, VT 05743
Evergreen Slate Company, 34 North Street, Granville, NY 12832

The Care and Splicing of Rope

by Earl W. Proulx

F AR OLDER THAN THE WHEEL, ROPE HAS BEEN AROUND almost as long as Man himself, an invaluable aid to his progress and industry. The earliest ropes were simply twisted vines, withes, creepers, or animal sinews. Eventually, men discovered how to twist plant fibers such as hemp, jute, flax, and cotton into "yarns;" yarns were in turn twisted together to form "strands," which were then twisted around each other (and sometimes, for extra strength, around a central core, or "heart") to form rope. Each element employs a different direction of twist — fibers are twisted right-handed to form yarns; yarns are laid left-handed into strands; and strands are laid right-handed into ropes (Fig. 1).

Particularly with a manila rope, these alternating twists must be kept in balance, so that the angle of lay is not shortened. Should that happen, the rope will kink, which bothers if you intend to use it in a pulley block, or indeed anywhere. To prevent this, uncoil your new rope straight out to its full length before using it at all, and drag it, pulling, along a clean ground. The rope's own weight will straighten out the balance and correct any shortening in the angle of lay. You may have to do this a few times before perfect balance is achieved.

Synthetic fibers such as nylon, Dacron, and polypropylene are widely used today for rope as well as the older materials.

The most durable natural-fiber rope is manila rope, made from the fibers of manila hemp. It is strong, has a low "stretch," i.e., does not grow much longer when loaded, and is easily spliced. A good manila rope will have been treated to resist water, mildew, and rot. The strongest rope made is nylon rope, which is very elastic, with a high stretch. Nylon rope will "relax," just as other ropes do, back to its original length

after being stretched. It splices as easily as manila, and will not kink, mildew, rot, or smell even when stored wet. Dacron rope is similar to nylon rope in strength, but closer to manila in stretch. It is generally preferred by yachtmen for running-rigging use over nylon, which is so elastic that it can alter the set of the sails. The high stretch of nylon, however, makes it an excellent mooring or anchor rope.

ROPE CARE

Treat a rope as a valuable tool. Do not drag it through the dirt or over sharp corners. If a single fiber is broken, the rope is weakened that much. Do not store rope wet, as it will mildew and rot. If a rope gets dirty, wash with clean water and dry out completely before storing, as dirt can weaken or cut strands and fibers. After washing, dry the rope uncoiled in the sun. Keep rope free from acids and chemicals.

Rope stored in a warm place such as a furnace room could be unsafe for heavy use. To check the inside fibers, partially untwist the strands to inspect their undersides. A dry, unheated room that has air circulation is the best place to store rope. Hang in loose coils on a wooden peg, never on a metal hook.

Keep in mind that smaller-diameter (up to ¾-inch) ropes will wear more rapidly than heavier ropes having a central core, because all the yarns in the former are exposed to surface wear.

A piece of twine can be broken with a snap, but not by pulling alone. The same thing applies to rope — a steady pull instead of a snap is the way to use it. A rope is weakened by knots. To form a knot the rope must be bent, and that brings most of the strain to bear on the outside fibers; this overloading breaks the outside fibers, increasing the load on the fibers beneath so that they too snap, and eventually the entire rope will break. It is therefore better to splice together two rope ends rather than knotting them. A knot weakens a rope by 50% but a splice has 95% of the breaking strength of the rope. All cut ends of a rope should be "whipped" to prevent the strands from unraveling.

WHIPPING

Ropes that are going to be passed through pulley blocks or halter ropes to be passed through small holes should have the ends whipped with strong twine.

This is done by freeing one strand of the rope back to where the whipping is to start (Fig. 2). Lay twine under this strand, leaving the end 10 to 12 inches long. Then relay the strand tightly as it was and wind the long end of the twine around the rope and the short end, being careful to pull it tight and also to keep each wind tight to the previous one. After about half the distance you plan to whip is covered, bend back the short end of the twine to form a loop reaching beyond the end of the rope. Then whip over both sides of the loop. Continue whipping as far as desired, then pass the long end through the loop and by pulling on the short end, draw the long end back halfway of the whipping and cut off both ends.

Fig. 1. *Rope is made by giving the fibers a right-handed twist to make yarns, the yarns being laid left-handed into strands, and the strands right-handed into ropes. The "lay" of a rope is the direction in which the strands are twisted. Most ropes are "right-hand," with the strands spiraling upward to the right when the rope is held vertically.*

FIBERS

YARNS

STRANDS

ROPE

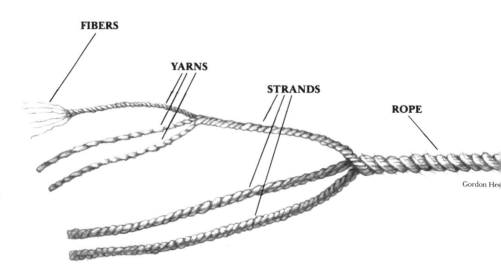

Gordon He

SPLICING

Splicing is a method of connecting two rope ends by unlaying the strands of each and then working them both up together to make one continuous rope. Splices should have approximately the same diameter as the rope itself, should be smooth and free from lumps, and should be made so that the tucks will not wear away and allow the rope to unstrand. A splice can be short or long, short being the strongest. The short splice can be used either to join the ends of two different ropes or to join the two ends of one length of rope — to form a rope ring. A "fid", or stout sharpened stick, is needed for this work.

Short Splice. Bind each rope about 12 inches from the end (at point A in Fig. 3). Unlay (untwist) the strands to this point.

Whip each strand to prevent unraveling (see above) and place the unraveled ends of each rope together as shown in the sketch, alternating the strands from each end. Pull together tightly. Temporarily, tie down all the strands together at point B, as shown in Figs. 3 and 4. Take off the initial binding (A) from one side of the rope and with the fid raise 1 strand on the same side (Fig. 4). Take the middle strand of the other side and tuck it over one strand and under the strand raised by the fid. Pull tight. This is known as a "tuck" (Fig. 5). Every time you tuck a strand, let the strand untwist a little, but be sure to keep tension on the raised strand under which you are tucking. This keeps the strands from kinking. In other words, a strand in the process of a tuck will pass over one twist of the second rope, under the next, raised by the fid, and out between the other two strands of its own rope. The tuck is always made in a direction opposite the lay, or twist, of the rope.

Roll the rope toward you as shown by the arrows in Fig. 6. Pick up the second strand and treat just as you did the first — over, under, and out. Roll the rope toward you again, and repeat the process with the third strand. You have now completed one *full* tuck. Now, make 3 more full tucks just like the first.

Cut off both temporary bindings (A and B, Fig. 7) from the other side of the rope. Tuck in this side the same as the other. If you tend to think in one direction, you can follow the same steps by simply reversing

the rope.

Cut off the ends of the strands, leaving 1 or 2 inches of strand protruding from the splice. Using the large end of your fid, pound down the splice and then roll it under your foot until it is tight.

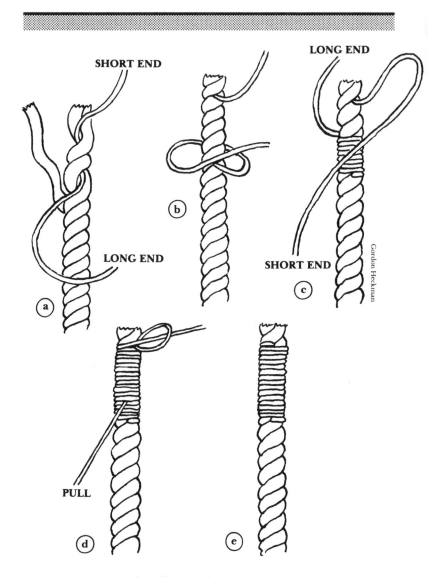

SHORT END

LONG END

LONG END

SHORT END

ⓐ ⓑ ⓒ

PULL

ⓓ ⓔ

Gordon Heckman

Fig. 2. *Whipping is a workmanlike way to bind the end of a rope that is to be passed, or "reeved," through holes or pulley blocks.*

To taper the splice, make the first two tucks on either end of the splice exactly as described above. For the third tuck, cut ⅓ of the yarn from each strand before proceeding with the tuck. Before making the fourth and final tuck, cut half of the remaining yarn from each strand. Finish the splice as described above (Fig. 8).

All synthetic ropes are spliced the same way as manila, except that one more full tuck must be made (5 in all).

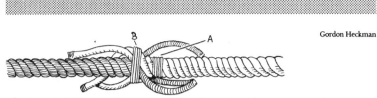

Gordon Heckman

Fig. 3. *Initial steps in making a short splice of two rope ends.*

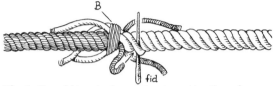

Fig. 4. *Use a fid to raise the rope loop in making the tuck.*

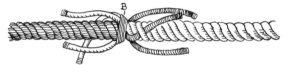

Fig. 5. *As you tuck each strand under and pull it tight, let out a little of its twist to prevent kinking.*

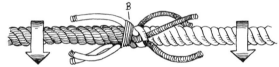

Fig. 6. *Roll the rope toward you before working another strand into the splice.*

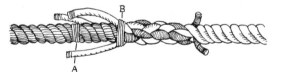

Fig. 7. *To work the other side of the splice, you may find it easier to reverse the rope rather than the directions.*

Fig. 8. *The completed short splice.*

FINALLY

When purchasing rope, keep the specific purpose or purposes for which it is to be used in mind. Knowing and practicing proper rope care is good economy, as a fine rope represents an investment — a ¾-inch manila or nylon rope sells for approximately $1 per foot — while larger-diameter ropes cost proportionately more.

Clock Repairs You Can Do Yourself

by Robert Wolf

A WISE MAN ONCE WROTE THAT JUDGMENTS ARE LIKE clocks: each is different, yet everyone believes his own. The world might be better if we could eliminate some of the differences in our judgments, but here we will deal only with clocks.

Over the centuries man has kept track of time in many ingenious ways. These include sundials, hourglasses, water clocks, and incense- and oil-burning timers. Clocks were first powered by weights; later, by steel springs, electricity, changes in the weather, even atomic energy. Power is usually regulated by pendulums, balance wheels, vibrations from tuning forks, or quartz crystals.

To me the best is not the newest. Unless you are riding a rocket to the moon, who cares whether your watch is accurate to 1 second a year? Isn't the primitive beauty of a New England steeple clock, the charm of a delicate pillar-and-scroll timepiece, or the homey grace of a simple cottage clock on the mantel more important?

I first became "hooked" on clocks when my mother handed me a nice octagonal wooden Connecticut wall clock with the observation that it would not run and I could do anything I liked with it. Well, I started by winding it and then shaking it, holding it in different positions, turning the hands, and pushing the balance wheel back and forth, but all to no avail. Then, concluding I had little to lose, I removed the hands and dial, took the movements out of the case, and a bit nervously inspected the maze of mysterious wheels, gears, and pinions. With beginner's luck, I happened to notice that a tooth of one particular gear was caught by a bent piece of metal on its opposite member, which was supposed to mesh with it. I pushed the bent metal back into place and, lo and behold, the clock started to tick away! What a beautiful sound!

Don't be afraid to tackle minor adjustments yourself. There are lots of constructive things you can do.

LOCATION

First, you have to decide where you are going to put your clock.

The best spot is on a wall or mantel where the clock can be firmly fixed in a level position. No clock will run well if frequently moved, whether accidentally or by an overzealous housekeeper. If practical, put a couple of screws through the back of the case into the wall.

Place your clock as far away as possible from suspected sources of dust (such as heating ducts and outlets), kitchen fumes, and the like. Make certain that the case of your clock is reasonably airtight. If the front or back door does not close properly, adjust the hinges or the latch to correct this. Some clocks have pulleys at the top around which the cord runs to the weights. It is a good idea to close pulley openings in the case by putting an empty wooden-match box tray (made to hold matches less than 2 inches long) on top of the case over each pulley.

Bracket. A nice bracket for your timepiece is quite easy to make. Cut a piece of ¾-inch clear pine about 2 inches longer and 2 inches deeper than the dimensions of the clock. If you like, you can nail and glue some attractive molding around the edges of the shelf, then cut out 2 supports on your jigsaw for the underside. A piece of the same clear pine about 1 inch high can be placed under the shelf, parallel to the back edge and long enough to fill the space between the 2 supports. The supports can be attached to each end of this piece. Some white glue reinforced with a few small brads and some wood stain to match the clock will finish the job. Two screws into the wall through the piece between the supports will hold the bracket securely in place.

Pendulums. Most antique clocks will have pendulums; if yours happens to have a balance wheel, just skip the parts of this discussion concerned with pendulums.

It is important that the pendulum produce a firm, even beat. There should be about the same time between each "tick" and "tock."

Listen carefully! If there is an unbalanced sound such that the clock produces a long silence after a hasty "tick-tock," adjustment is called for. The simplest way to fix this is to raise one side of the clock so as to tip it toward the silent side. If the clock has legs, you might place a few pennies under them on one side of the clock until the beat evens out. If you have a shelf clock without legs, fold some paper so that it is about an inch wide, a bit shorter than the depth of the clock (in this way the paper will not be visible), and as thick as needed to raise the side of the clock for the desired sound. A little trial and error will nearly always solve the situation. Needless to say, these adjustments should be made before permanently fastening the clock to the wall with screws.

Crutch. Once in a while you will find that to get a nice, even beat you have to raise one side of the clock so high that the entire case is obviously way out of line and aesthetically unacceptable. In this event, you will have to adjust the "crutch." This is the U-shaped piece on the wire connecting the pendulum rod to the movement (Fig. 2). By bending the wire to which the crutch is attached slightly to one side or the other, you can change the beat of the pendulum without moving the clock case. For instructions on how to expose the crutch to make this adjustment, see below.

In positioning your clock, you must be certain that the front-to-back level of the clock is such that neither the pendulum bob nor the pendulum rod makes contact with the case while swinging back and forth. Also, the rod should not rub against either end of the crutch but should ride freely midway in the crutch.

Put your ear close to the case while the pendulum is swinging and listen for any sound of friction. If there is any question, the best procedure is to inspect the mechanism both while the pendulum is stationary and while it is in motion. To do this, carefully pull out the pin in the center of the dial (a small pair of flat-nosed pliers will be helpful), lift the washer holding the hands (sometimes the washer will be threaded and hence must be unscrewed), and then lift off the minute and hour hands straight up at a right angle to the dial so as not to bend them. The dial can then be taken off by removing the screws or pins or by turning the L-shaped nails that hold it in place. The clock should now be permanently positioned so that the pendulum rod is about in the middle of the crutch while it rests and does not hit the case while swinging. As noted above, the crutch can be gently bent from one side or the other to even out the beat if raising one side of the clock does not do this satisfactorily.

When replacing the dial, hands, washer, and pin, put all of the parts back exactly as they were or you may have trouble getting everything to fit. Be sure to point the hour and minute hands to the same time as when you disassembled them (otherwise the striking mechanism may not be coordinated with the time). If by chance the pin should break and you have no replacement handy, you can use a short piece of wire or a small nail with the ends snipped off with wire cutters.

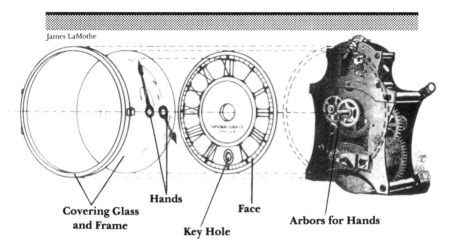

James LaMothe

Covering Glass and Frame — **Hands** — **Face** — **Key Hole** — **Arbors for Hands**

Fig. 1. *Exploded view of covering glass and frame, minute and hour hands, face, keyhole, and arbors for hands of mantel clock.*

FAST-SLOW ADJUSTMENTS

If your clock is running consistently too fast or too slow, a simple adjustment of the pendulum bob is probably all that is needed. The shorter the length of the pendulum, the faster the clock will go, and vice versa. Therefore to speed up the timepiece, turn the small nut underneath the pendulum bob one full turn clockwise and let the clock run for a while to check on its accuracy. Repeat this adjustment once each day until no longer required. To slow things down, do just the reverse.

If your clock has a balance wheel and not a pendulum, there will be a fast-slow adjustment lever with the letters "F" and "S" to tell you which way to move it. On European clocks these letters may be "A" and "R," standing for "advance" and "retard." Moving this lever has the same effect as shortening or lengthening the pendulum, because it does just that to the hairspring which controls the balance wheel.

PROBLEMS

Dirt is your clock's chief enemy. If it gets into the movement, it mixes with the clock oil to form an abrasive gum that can cause wear and poor time keeping. Eventually it will stop the clock altogether.

If the clock is stopping, notice whether this happens at the identical time each day. Perhaps one of the hands is making contact as it passes by the other, or with the dial plate or with the glass cover over the dial. You have undoubtedly heard the expression, "a face that would stop a clock" — this can be literally true. The clock may be stopping only when the hand arrives at the same trouble spot each day. The remedy is simply to adjust the offending hand by bending it carefully so that the unwanted contact is eliminated.

Sometimes the weight that drives your clock may be hitting a projection on its way down in the case. Naturally, the movement will

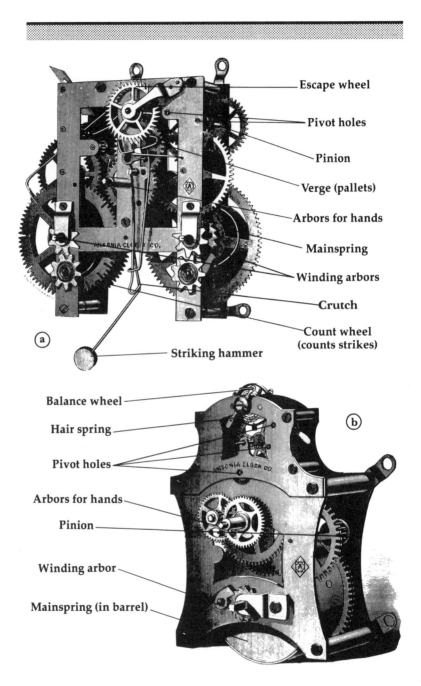

Escape wheel

Pivot holes

Pinion

Verge (pallets)

Arbors for hands

Mainspring

Winding arbors

Crutch

Count wheel
(counts strikes)

Striking hammer

Balance wheel

Hair spring

Pivot holes

Arbors for hands

Pinion

Winding arbor

Mainspring (in barrel)

Fig. 2. a) *Movement of 8-day pendulum clock.* b) *Movement of 8-day lever or balance-wheel clock. Reproduced from 1880 Ansonia Clock Company catalog courtesy of the American Clock and Watch Museum, Inc., Bristol, Connecticut.*

then halt because the weight cannot fall freely in its channel. The trick here is to detect the malfunction — the cure is obvious, namely removing or covering the projection.

Another trouble spot is the pulley over which the cord passes from the weight to the movement. The cord may have come off the pulley or the axle holding the pulley may have come loose from its bearing. Again the problem is to discover the difficulty.

One of the most common troubles is lack of lubrication. This results from long use or — even faster — from nonuse, which may cause the oil to run out and dry up. Here let me warn you that if your clock is very dirty it may be better not to try to oil it and get it to run, because the dirt can cause friction, wear out the pivots, gears, and pinions, and result in a bigger repair job. Please don't do what a friend of mine tried: he took out the movement, doused it in kerosene, and then replaced it to find, of course, that absolutely nothing was working. A really dusty clock will have to be dismantled, cleaned in *clock-cleaning solution,* reassembled, and then oiled. This should be done by a competent clock repairman.

If your clock is not too dirty, it may need just a bit of lubricant to go on ticking for several years. To do the job you must use clock oil — not motor oil, sewing-machine oil, salad oil, household oil, 3-in-1 oil — but *clock* oil. This is made specially for the purpose, and will not attract dust, get gummy, or dry out too quickly. You can buy clock oil at any jewelry-supply house. If you have difficulty finding one, write to S. LaRose, Inc., Greensboro, NC 27420, and ask for their latest catalogue ($2.50 at this writing), listing all kinds of interesting clock parts and accessories. To apply the oil, you can use a specially made clock oiler or a fine toothpick, a long thin nail, a piece of wire, or any similar object. I use an old dentist's pick.

Take off the hands and dial. Place a very small amount of the oil where the holes are in the plates of the clock, on the pendulum rod where it passes through the crutch, on all sides of the verge or escapement (this will usually be in the approximate shape of an upside-down V, located near the top of the clock and rocking back and forth as the pendulum swings), on the pin that holds the verge in place, on the mainspring, and on the axles holding the pulleys around which the cords pass from the weights to the movement. Use the oil sparingly — too much will attract dust. About 2 drops of the oil should be enough for the entire job. If your clock has a balance wheel, do not let oil get on the hairspring, which turns the balance wheel. And, if you happen to have a wooden-works movement, do not oil the wood because this will make it swell up and stop the clock; here oil only the metal pendulum rod at the crutch and the metal verge and its pin.

GENERAL MAINTENANCE

Wind your clock regularly — that is, about the same time each day (or each week, if you have a so-called 8-day movement). Be gentle, and do not overwind. This can break a spring or snap a cord holding the weight. If your clock has a heavy weight, it is a good practice to assist the winding process by supporting the weight from underneath with one hand while winding with the other. Also, take a look once in a while at the cord holding the weight to check that it is not frayed. Replacing it with nylon cord is well worth the trouble and will reduce the possibility of damage from a broken cord and a falling weight.

When resetting the hands of your clock, do not push them backward. With many movements, this can damage the mechanism. Advance the minute hand (the longer one) gently to the desired time, pausing for the striking mechanism to complete its cycle before hurrying on past each hour (or half or quarter hour, if your clock also strikes here). If you wish to set the time back 1 hour, such as when changing from daylight-saving to standard time, do not push the hands backward. However, instead of advancing 11 hours, all you have to do is stop your clock for 1 hour and then start it again.

To discuss striking mechanisms in any detail would take us into the complexities of many arrangements to which uniform instructions would not apply. However, if your clock is striking a number different from that indicated by the hands, one solution is to push the hour hand (the shorter one) gently so that it points to the number sounded by the strike. (This can be done on most clocks without damage, but should the hour hand be extremely hard to advance, don't force it.) Then reset the hands of your clock forward to the proper time, allowing the clock to strike each hour along the way. Should you wish to learn more about the details of clock repairing, collecting, buying, and selling clocks, the theory and history of time keeping, and descriptions of all the different types of escapements, striking, calendar and repeating mechanisms, and the like, I have two suggestions.

First, join the National Association of Watch and Clock Collectors, Inc. (address at this writing: NAWCC, P.O. Box 33, Columbia, PA 17512). This nonprofit organization now has over 30,000 members with local chapters all over the country, including one in New England. The nominal annual membership fee includes subscriptions to an excellent bimonthly bulletin and every in-between month to a "Mart" with lists of horological items both wanted and for sale. The publications of this organization and its chapter meetings provide the best possible sources of education and opportunities to buy watches and clocks of all descriptions and prices. If you purchase from a dealer, the price naturally has to include a healthy amount for his overhead and profit. Buying from a fellow collector may be less expensive and more fun. My second suggestion is to send for the latest book catalogue issued by Adams Brown Co., Box 357, Cranbury, NJ 08517. You will receive a complete list and description of over 200 literary works covering all aspects of the field.

Preserving Meats and Vegetables by Salting, Brining, and Pickling

by Barbara Radcliffe Rogers

CERTAINLY AMONG THE OLDEST AND MOST PRIMITIVE ways of reliably preserving meats and vegetables, salting, brining, and pickling have given the world some of its favorite dishes.

MEAT

These techniques give their own distinctive flavors to meats; none of these processes is difficult or even very time consuming, though long since replaced by more efficient means of long-term storage. Corned beef, pickled herring, pickled pigs' feet, and spiced beef remain popular specialty meats. Salt pork is still a staple ingredient in everything from snap beans to apple pie.

Before you begin brining, it is wise to mosey about the far reaches of your home with a thermometer in hand. Make a note of the temperature of your cellar (and every corner thereof), bulkhead, attic, sheds, and any unheated section of your home during the cold months. Then, when you need a place to store full crocks, you'll know right where to go.

If you have brined foods stored in such places and the temperature falls well below freezing for a sustained period, check your crocks often and move them to a slightly warmer spot until the weather turns.

Salt Pork. Nothing could be easier than making salt pork. We use the dry salting method on the thin cuts such as fatback. For our use, we cut the pieces in 4-inch to 6-inch slabs. For 12 pounds we use ½ pound of pickling salt and ¼ cup brown sugar.

Coat all the pieces, using all the salt mixture. Sterilize a 2-gallon crock or two 1-gallon glass jars and let them cool. To sterilize a stoneware crock, wash and rinse it well in *hot* water. Boil a sufficient quantity of water to fill the crock twice. Pour boiling water into crock, letting it overflow a little. Let stand 5 minutes, empty out water (be careful!), and repeat. Pack the meat tightly in crock or jars, and cover with cheesecloth tied on tight.

Keep it at 36°F. (no higher than 38°F., and no lower than freezing) for at least a month (a cold cellar is perfect). Wrap salt pork in moisture-proof paper or plastic wrap and keep in a cold place (36°F.) or in your freezer. It will keep all winter.

There is another method just as reliable, which calls for a brine. Pack the cut pieces in a sterilized crock or in glass jars and cover with a brine of 3 quarts water, 1 pound pickling salt, and ½ cup brown sugar. Be sure the salt and sugar are dissolved.

The brine must cover every inch of meat. Weight it down with a plate and a heavy object such as a canning jar full of water. Cover the container and store a week at 36° to 38°F.

Remove the meat, stir the brine, and repack meat each week for 4 weeks. If at any time the brine seems thick or stringy, wash each piece of meat thoroughly, resterilize the container, and mix fresh brine.

The pork may be left in the brine — although it will be very salty — or it may be dried, wrapped, and frozen. No Yankee (or Southerner, either) needs to be told how to use salt pork, but I'll include my father-in-law's favorite vegetable dish because it's so good and because I've never seen it anywhere but at our houses. He had it once on Cape Cod, analyzed it with a chemist's accuracy as he ate, and reproduced the dish when he came home. We've always called it Cape Cod Dish. Here's how my mother-in-law makes it.

Norm Rogers' Cape Cod Dish

1 pound freshly shelled green peas
1 pound fresh snapped green beans
¼ pound salt pork, chopped
1 pint heavy cream
salt and pepper

Boil 2 cups of water in each of two saucepans and divide salt pork between them. Simmer 10 minutes and then add peas to one pan, beans to the other. Cook gently until each is just tender. If one finishes before the other, set it aside to wait. When both are done, combine them, with just enough of the liquid so as to not quite cover. Add the cream, heat very carefully so the cream doesn't boil, and adjust seasonings. Serve hot. *Serves 6.*

This same basic recipe can be used with either vegetable alone or with corn instead. If you use corn and add potatoes and onions, you have a splendid corn chowder.

Pickled Pigs' Feet. Pigs' feet are another type of cured meat that derives from a time when every scrap of meat was preserved and eaten; they are now expensive deli-shelf items.

Wash the feet thoroughly, sprinkle with salt, and leave overnight. Wash again and boil until tender, but not falling apart.

Make a pickling solution of 2 quarts of white vinegar, 1 hot red pepper, 2 bay leaves, 1 tablespoon peppercorns, 1 teaspoon cloves, and a few whole allspice. Bring to a boil. To can, pack feet in sterile canning jars and cover with vinegar solution leaving ½ inch of headspace. Process pints and quarts 1¾ hours at 10 pounds pressure. *Do not can pigs' feet if you don't have a pressure canner.* Or, you can simply pack the feet in jars in the pickling solution and store in the refrigerator for several weeks safely.

Pickled Herring. Pickled herring are an old favorite wherever fish are plentiful. Cut off heads and thin belly flesh from fresh, thoroughly cleaned herring. Remove dark vein next to the spine. Wash well and drain. Pack in loose, criss-crossed layers in a sterile crock or jar.

Make a pickle of 1 quart white vinegar, 1 quart water, and a generous ½ cup pickling salt. Pour over fish to cover and weight down well. Leave fish 4 days if they are small, and as long as a week if large. Check daily. If the skin begins to fade or wrinkle, remove fish.

Cut fish crosswise into one-inch slices. *Resterilize crock* and pack fish in layers alternating with sliced red onions, fresh dill sprigs, a sliced carrot, a few bay leaves, and a sprinkling of pickling spice.

Combine 1 quart white vinegar, ½ cup brown sugar, 1 cup water, 1 tablespoon allspice, 1 tablespoon mustard seed, and 1 tablespoon black peppercorns and bring to a boil. Cool and pour over herring. Refrigerate one week before using. These will keep six months in a tightly closed jar in the refrigerator.

Corned Beef. The basis for the traditional boiled dinner, corned beef is equally good served as hash or sandwich meat. There are many recipes for corning beef, but I like a fairly spicy one.

Use brisket, round, or chuck (brisket is good and has few other uses). Pack the pieces of meat in a sterile crock or jar, using a pound of pickling salt for 10 pounds of meat. Put salt in the bottom, rub each piece well, and sprinkle salt between layers and on top. Let stand 24 hours.

Dissolve 1 cup pickling salt, ½ cup brown sugar, 1 tablespoon sodium nitrate (saltpeter), and 1 teaspoon baking soda in 1 gallon of warm water. Add 2 tablespoons pickling spice, 2 teaspoons paprika, a dozen bay leaves, and 4 garlic cloves. Cool and pour over meat in crock. Cover with a plate and weight down so that *all* the meat is covered. Let cure 8 weeks at 34° to 38°F.

Each week, turn meat and check brine. If it is thick or stringy, pour it off, wash meat well, resterilize container, and make a new brine using *2 cups* of salt (to replace the salt you packed the meat in).

You can omit the saltpeter if you are opposed to it, but your meat will be gray instead of pink. Before you do omit it, read the section entitled "Nitrate Worry" in *Putting Food By*, by Ruth Hertzberg, Beatrice Vaughan, and Janet Greene (see *References*).

Spiced Beef. An old English favorite for Christmas, spiced beef has a distinctive flavor and is served sliced very thin as a first course or as a nibbling meat with common crackers or buttered, fresh bread.

Cover a 4-pound beef brisket with ¼ cup dark brown sugar, pressing it in firmly. Place in a covered dish and keep in a cold place (the refrigerator is fine) for 2 days.

Crush together ¼ cup whole juniper berries, 2 tablespoons whole allspice, 1 tablespoon black peppercorns, and ¼ cup pickling salt. Each day for 2 weeks press about 2 teaspoons of the spice mixture onto the surface of the meat and return, covered, to a cold place.

After 2 weeks, wash beef under running water to remove spices, place in casserole, and add 1 cup water. Bake at 275°F., covered, for 3 to 4 hours or until meat is very tender.

Cool to room temperature and wrap in plastic wrap. Put meat on a flat plate, cover with a board or plate, and weight with about 5 pounds. Refrigerate 24 hours, weighted. Remove weight and store the meat, tightly wrapped, in refrigerator. It will keep for a month.

VEGETABLES

Although the practice of putting down the summer's bounty of vegetables in crocks has given way largely to canning and freezing, the end products of brining simply can't be duplicated by either.

Sauerkraut, crisp sweet pickles, salted sweet corn, and a variety of dill-pickled vegetables are prepared entirely in a brining crock. The procedure is not nearly as uncertain as rumor holds it to be. If directions are followed, success is almost certain.

Before you are discouraged by the scarcity and price of good stoneware crocks, let me explain that by "crock" I mean not only the old pottery ones, but any unchipped enamel pot or large glass jar. One works just as well as another as long as the basic rules are followed. The gallon, wide-mouth jars that restaurants buy pickles in work beautifully. They may not look like Grandma's but the taste of the sauerkraut will be just as good.

Should you have an old crock, don't use it for brining or pickling if there is a white film on the inside that disappears when wet and reappears upon drying. The crock has been used for waterglassing eggs. There is no way to remove that coating, and it will ruin your pickles. Likewise, once you have used a stoneware crock for brining, don't make wine in it.

The only magic rules in brining, apart from the strength of the brine, are to keep your hands and any metal object out of the jar or crock. The old jingle "a hand in the pot spoils the lot" is true, and a metal spoon will do just as much damage. Use wooden spoons and mashers and glass or crockery for dipping and weighting.

The best and freshest ingredients will yield the best product. Put your old, tough cabbage and your not so freshly picked cucumbers through the grinder and make relish. But use young, fresh, tender cabbage for kraut and fresh-picked (within four hours) cucumbers for pickles.

Sauerkraut. Sauerkraut made at home has no peer in a can or at a deli counter. For a 1-gallon container, core and shred 5 pounds of cabbage. Measure out 3 tablespoons of pickling (or kosher or dairy) salt. (Never use iodized table salt.)

Alternate layers of cabbage with a sprinkling of salt, tapping each layer with a wooden potato masher (or the end of a short length of 2x4 covered with cheesecloth). The top layer should be salt.

This will not seem like enough salt, but it will give you a 2½ percent solution, the right strength for fermentation.

Boil an old dish towel or piece of sheeting for 5 minutes and cover the crock with it. Weight this down with a flat plate the size of the inside of the crock and weight the plate with a canning jar full of water. If you are using a glass pickle jar, you will not need so much weight and the empty jar alone will suffice.

If your cabbage was fresh and tender, by the next day you should have enough brine to cover the cabbage. If you don't, make more brine in the proportion of 1½ teaspoons of salt to a cup of water and add enough to cover.

In 2 or 3 days, white scum will form on the top. Skim this off, replace the cloth with a newly boiled one, wash the plate, and replace it all. Repeat this skimming (a 5-minute job) each day until the bubbles stop rising. Then your sauerkraut is done; it takes about 2 weeks.

At this point, simply keep the cabbage below the brine with the plate, cover the crock tightly, and store at 40° to 50°F. If your cellar isn't that cool, heat the kraut just to simmering, pack in canning jars, seal, and process in a water bath 20 minutes for quarts, 15 minutes for pints.

If you have made only 1 gallon, you will have no problem storing it because it won't last very long.

Salted Sweet Corn. Dry salting without fermenting is a last-ditch stand for most vegetables because they lose so much in texture and food value. But there is one exception: salted sweet corn is a dish all its own and, if you have corn to spare, worth sampling.

Use good, fresh corn at the height of its season. Husk and steam it on the cob for 10 minutes. Cut off from the cob and weigh. Using 1 part salt to 4 parts corn, layer the two in a crock as you did the cabbage. Follow the same procedure, adding more brine (3 tablespoons of salt to a cup of water) if necessary.

Since there is no fermentation, you don't have to skim. Store the crock at 37° to 45°F., and in about a month you can begin dipping out what you need for supper (use a glass or china cup).

To serve, soak in several baths of cold water until a sample bite does not taste salty. Cook in very little water until tender, and serve with butter. This corn also makes excellent chowder.

Preserved Peppers. Green peppers may be preserved whole in a brine made from 1 pound of pickling salt to 2 quarts of water. (Heat the water to dissolve the salt, then allow to cool before using.) Keep peppers submerged with a weighted plate. Freshen as with corn and use at any time for stuffed peppers or in cooking.

Dill Pickles. A dill crock is still the best way to make high quality, crisp dill pickles, either with whole very fresh cucumbers, or with a variety of other vegetables.

Make a brine of ¾ cup of pickling salt, 2½ quarts of water, and ½ cup of vinegar, heating to dissolve salt and cooling before use. Alternate layers of vegetables — cucumbers, cauliflower pieces, green- and red-pepper strips, onions (sliced or small whole), sliced green tomatoes, summer squash, baby ears of corn — with layers of fresh dill. You may want to add hot red peppers and peeled garlic cloves for a pickle with more character.

Pour brine over vegetables, and weight down using a cloth, plate, and weight, removing scum daily as with sauerkraut. In 2 weeks, pack vegetables in hot sterile jars. Heat ½ cup pickling salt, 1 quart vinegar, and 4 quarts water to boiling, pour over vegetables, and seal. Process 15 minutes in boiling-water bath.

Sweet Pickles. For an excellent sweet pickle, put 2 dozen 3-inch cucumbers, freshly picked, in a crock or jar. Cover with a brine of ½ cup pickling salt, ¼ cup vinegar, and 2 quarts water. Cover, weight, and skim daily as with sauerkraut. After 2 weeks, drain, cut in chunks, and let stand 24 hours in cold water. Rinse.

Combine 3 cups vinegar with 6 cups of sugar and ½ cup water. Tie 2 tablespoons each whole cloves and mixed pickling spices in cheesecloth, add to vinegar solution, and bring to a boil. Pour over cucumbers and let stand 24 hours. Drain, reheat syrup, and repeat four times. (This is a 5-minute process each day.)

Remove spices and pack pickles in sterile jars. Bring syrup to boil and pour over pickles. Seal and process in boiling water bath 10 minutes.

There are other variations on the pickling and brining crock. The Koreans make a kraut of cabbage, garlic, and red-hot peppers, which they bury all winter. By spring the kraut is so hot that it melts the snow above it, and thus is easily located. The Japanese make a tasty brined pickle of carrots, cucumbers, white radish, and eggplant.

Following the basic directions above, you can experiment to create your very own vegetable crock . . . and never be caught meatless when the power goes off!

REFERENCES

Putting Food By, by Ruth Hertzberg, Beatrice Vaughan, and Janet Greene (The Stephen Greene Press, Brattleboro, VT, 1973).

Reclaiming an Overgrown Field

by Jay Jacobs

T HE OLD FIELD ON YOUR PROPERTY — THAT NEGLECTED eyesore overgrown with weeds and brush and good for exactly nothing — need not stay that way forever. It can be reclaimed with time and effort, at reasonable expense, depending on the purpose you wish to serve. Most time-consuming and expensive is a hay field, but then the hay harvest is a saleable, renewable asset. Less costly is a pasture, fenced and reseeded, and least expensive of all is a purely scenic field, cleared but not fenced. (You can always put it to work later on.)

A hay field may be the right choice where the land and soil conditions are suitable, and if you have, or have access to, the equipment (mower, rake, tedder or conditioner, baler, etc.) required. In most areas of the country, you have some options on how to handle the hay field: you may give the hay from the field for a few years to a farmer in exchange for his underwriting and providing all necessary tillage, fertil-

izer, lime, seed, and harvest of the crop; or you can sell the standing hay (stumpage) to a buyer who will do his own cutting and baling. You can hire someone to custom cut and bale the hay for you to store, either to feed your own animals or to sell; or, of course, you can do all the work yourself — if you have the time and the equipment.

Whatever you decide, gather as much practical and technical advice as you can from others before embarking on your reclaiming project. Sources such as your County Cooperative Extension Service, the County Soil and Water Conservation District, or a local farmer can give you a good idea of fertilizer, lime, and seed required, the overall costs, when to do what, and how best to carry out the various operations involved. Ask lots of questions and take every chance you can to see what others have done.

The first step is to take a soil sample from your field and have it tested to measure the pH (level of acidity or alkalinity) and the content of available phosphorus, potash, and magnesium. Get a clean pail and spade, and dig a slice of earth 6 to 8 inches deep from each of 4 to 6 spots per acre. Crumble all the slices together in the pail, mix well, and fill a paper cup with the soil mixture. Label the cup with your name and address, and bring or send it to your County Extension Agent (or to a fertilizer dealer) to be tested. The agent or dealer will process the sample and advise what your soil needs, based on the test results.

The fall and winter months are a good time to begin clearing your field back to the original boundaries or walls. (The stone walls common in New England were built from the rocks picked out of the fields. As practical as they are handsome, stone walls merit preservation and maintenance. See *The Forgotten Art of Building a Stone Wall*, by Curtis P. Fields, Yankee Publishing Incorporated, 1971.) With brush saw, chain saw, axe, clippers, and pole-saw pruner, cut out all brush, young or unwanted trees, burdocks, brambles, and overhanging branches. When felling trees, cut the stumps close to the ground whether you intend to leave them to rot or plan to have them removed by bulldozer or backhoe. In the former case, score the upper surfaces of the stumps with the chain saw to hasten decomposition. Or pile brush on top and burn (with permission from your local fire department). In the latter case, stumps are cut low so as not to hamper the maneuverability of the machine. Cut stumps high only if they are to be pulled out with a winch or tractor.

As spring approaches and the snow recedes, mark rocks or stumps to be removed before new brush and grass grow up to hide them. Fencing should be done as soon as the frost is out and the ground is soft, facilitating post-hole digging and post setting. Then, too, you can let animals out on the field in the spring prior to plowing and planting. This practice helps get rid of unwanted growth and weeds and is particularly valuable should you plan to frost seed (page 54) without plowing. The most effective animals for the purpose are pigs, sheep, or goats. The more animals on the field, the less time it will take them to overgraze it right down to the bare earth in places — the fewer animals, the longer the time. When most of the vegetation is gone and the bare spots appear, the field is ready for plowing or frost seeding.

The old timers preferred to use pigs, which will not only "plow" the field by rooting but actually aid in stump removal. If a little grain is buried among the roots of a stump, pigs will root up the stump to get at the grain!

For fencing you will need 7-foot posts of white or red cedar or pressure-treated pine, about 4 inches in diameter. Dig holes 24 to 30 inches deep to leave enough post above ground to hold a standard 4-foot woven-wire fence topped with 6-inch boards. The large end of the post goes in the ground, and should be firmly tamped down. Posts should be spaced 10 to 12 feet apart. Should you plan a barbed-wire or electric fence, instead of digging post holes you can make 18-inch pilot holes with an iron crowbar, insert sharpened posts (2 to 3 inches in diameter) into the holes, and drive them into the ground with a maul or sledgehammer.

As the ground dries out, start removing stumps and rocks. This is especially important for a hay field, because any stump or rock left in represents a potential hazard to expensive equipment. The fewer rocks and stumps left in a field, the more closely it can be clipped or mowed. If there are a lot of rocks or stumps, it might be best to hire a bulldozer or backhoe. But if you are long on time, patience, and energy, you can work out most rocks and stumps yourself, using a crowbar, ⅜-inch logging chain, horse, tractor, or 4-wheel drive truck, and a stone boat.

To determine the size of a rock, strike it with the crowbar. A high, piercing ring usually indicates a large rock; a duller sound, a rock you should be able to handle. Dig around the stump or rock enough to slide the logging chain around it. The chain should be under a root or lip and then hooked back into itself with the slip hook, causing a noose around the rock. A slow steady pull by truck, tractor, or horse is best. You may have to change the position of the chain several times before dislodging the obstacle. With a stump, you'll probably have to chop off the bigger roots before it will come out.

Although you can try using a snowplow (if you have one on your truck) to push the rocks and stumps off the field, a stone boat is probably more practical and is easily built. The boat should be constructed of 2x8-inch hardwood boards, and should be about 3 feet wide by 8 feet long (Fig. 1). Buy the curved steel headpiece at a farm-equipment store, or have one made of ½- to ⅜-inch steel plate, with the nose bent up like a ski tip. Bolt the headpiece to the front ends of the boards with ½-inch carriage bolts. You can bolt lengths of 2x4-inch boards on top of the planks along either long edge to keep stones from jouncing off the boat over rough ground, but these are not necessary.

Pull the boat up beside the rock or stump to be loaded and either lever it on with the crowbar or drag it on with truck, tractor, or horse

Chris Tremblay

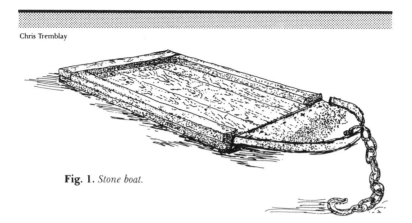

Fig. 1. *Stone boat.*

power. Hitch the stone boat to your pulling power and tow the load where you want it.

Although letting animals on to the field before plowing and reseeding will greatly reduce unwanted growth, pernicious weeds such as milkweed, Canada thistle, or burdock must be clipped back annually before they flower and drop seed. Ideally, they should be dug up by the roots and burned.

Seeding the field is a most important step and must be done correctly. When to plant will depend on the type of seed chosen and on the preparation of the land. For best results, the land should be plowed and disc-harrowed in spring or fall. Then apply lime and fertilizer (as specified by the results of the soil test), and disc these in well, going over the land with the harrow until the soil is loose and friable.

THE CYCLONE SEEDER

Fig. 2. *Seeder.*

For the actual sowing, use a Cyclone hand seeder (Fig. 2). For suggested seed mixtures and amounts per acre of hay field or pasture, see the Table below. After the seed has been broadcast, scratch it in with a brush drag made from a number of young (2-inch diameter) birch or similarly brushy trees tied together, pulling the drag over the seeded field. Seed planted as outlined above will have the highest germination rate, with just a slight edge given to fall planting, when the seed will meet less competition from weeds.

Much less expensive and much less effort — though also less productive — is frost seeding. Apply lime and fertilizer on top of the field in the fall and pasture or clip closely so that ground is largely clear of

TABLE OF HAY AND PASTURE SEED MIXTURES, WITH SEED RATES

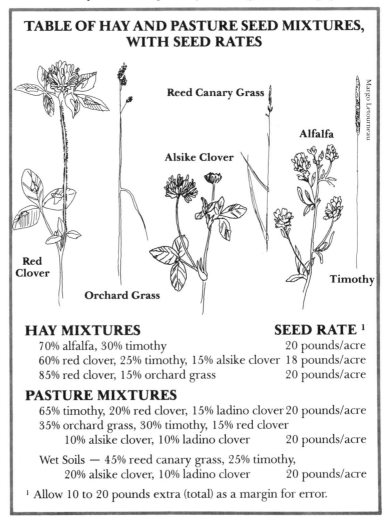

Reed Canary Grass

Alfalfa

Alsike Clover

Red Clover

Orchard Grass

Timothy

Margo Letourneau

HAY MIXTURES   SEED RATE [1]

70% alfalfa, 30% timothy	20 pounds/acre
60% red clover, 25% timothy, 15% alsike clover	18 pounds/acre
85% red clover, 15% orchard grass	20 pounds/acre

PASTURE MIXTURES

65% timothy, 20% red clover, 15% ladino clover	20 pounds/acre
35% orchard grass, 30% timothy, 15% red clover 10% alsike clover, 10% ladino clover	20 pounds/acre
Wet Soils — 45% reed canary grass, 25% timothy, 20% alsike clover, 10% ladino clover	20 pounds/acre

[1] Allow 10 to 20 pounds extra (total) as a margin for error.

vegetation. In early spring, when the snow has mostly gone and the frost is coming out of the ground, keep your eyes peeled for cracks in the earth — random, weblike patterns similar to those seen in drought-parched areas. (You can usually see them in your driveway, if it is dirt.) Watch carefully, because the appearance of these cracks means that it is time to sow the frost seeding — NOW! This is because at this brief stage in the seasonal cycle, seed broadcast over the ground with the Cyclone hand seeder will come to rest within these cracks. In New England, this will be somewhere between late March and the end of April. Success is variable, as germination depends on moist soil conditions and frequent showers (even of snow), and the seed-to-soil contact is nothing like that afforded by plowing, discing, and scratching as described above. However, sowing at the "crack" stage will give you maximal contact for this method. You will require approximately 1½ times the amount of seed specified for conventional plantings. Despite these drawbacks, frost seeding is convenient and can be used any spring to reseed bare spots caused by winterkill or overgrazing.

A word about the seed itself. Basically, there are three types of seed: legumes, grasses, and small grains. Nitrogen-fixing legumes, which draw the nitrogen they need from the atmosphere and store it in nodules on their root systems and thus do not require expensive nitrogen fertilizer, are alfalfa and clover. Alfalfa requires a high (6.2 to 7.0) soil pH, and costs up to $3 per *pound*. Alfalfa hay is very rich and is better for cows than for horses. Clovers are less expensive and need a lower soil pH; they work well in reclaiming a field. Clovers must be reseeded every 2 to 3 years to keep them strong.

Grasses for your purpose include timothy, brome grass, orchard grass, and reed canary grass, the latter for wet areas. Orchard grass is a good choice for frost seeding — it is relatively inexpensive and, once established, regenerates easily. Timothy and brome are popular hay grasses.

Small grains include winter rye, oats, and barley. These make excellent cover crops to prevent soil erosion, and can be plowed back into the ground as "green manure" to increase soil fertility. As annuals, small grains must be reseeded every year.

A neglected, overgrown field is a challenge, while a reclaimed field — cleared, resown, and regrown — is its own reward. But in between there can be some headaches. Minimize problems by thinking out the project as a whole before doing anything. Don't think too big — a couple of acres is a good size — and be prepared for the expense involved; seed, fertilizer, and lime can cost over $200 per acre. Know how you will handle the plowing and harrowing, and, if you decide on a mowing field, the hay harvest. Then, in a couple of years, you will have gained a new and useful asset, as well as a decidedly improved view.

Making a Rope Hammock

by Sidne Lewis

ALTHOUGH MAKING A HAMMOCK LOOKS LIKE A TRE-mendous undertaking, in fact only three basic knots are re-quired to make a handsome and comfortable one — namely, the overhand knot, the half hitch, and the square knot. If you have never worked with rope before, practice making these 3 knots with short lengths of rope before beginning your hammock. An overhand knot is the simplest knot of all, whether made with a single cord (Fig. 3) or with double cords (Fig. 4). A single half hitch is scarcely a knot at all, being essentially an underhand loop (Fig. 1) made around a support, but when repeated to form a double or triple half hitch it becomes a knot that will hold (Fig. 2). The familiar square knot known to every one-time Boy or Girl Scout will be made for this purpose around other cords, so learn this macramé procedure (Fig. 5) before beginning your hammock. Properly tied, a square knot will lie flat and will tie and untie easily. A "granny," or improperly tied square knot, will not lie flat, and tends to either jam or slip. Avoid "grannies"!

For an overhand knot, make an overhand loop (Fig. 1), then pass the free end under and through the loop: right over left, under and through — or, left over right, under and through (Fig. 3). A double-cord overhand knot (Fig. 4) is made exactly like the single cord knot, with the 2 cords knotted as one.

To tie a triple half hitch (Fig. 2), make an underhand loop around the support (holding cord or bar). Pass the free end around the holding cord or bar and through the loop formed by so doing. This is the first hitch. For the second half hitch, pass the free end around the support and through the loop as before — then repeat once more for the third half hitch. Push the knot up against the support.

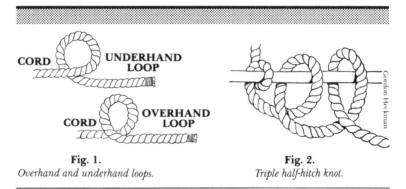

Fig. 1.
Overhand and underhand loops.

Fig. 2.
Triple half-hitch knot.

To tie a macramé square knot over 1 or 2 cords, proceed as follows. (The example shown in Fig. 5 is tied over 2 cords; the procedure is exactly the same if the knot is to be tied over a single cord. In the directions that follow, call this single cord "BC.") Mentally label the 4 cords from left to right in sequence "A," "B," "C," and "D" (Fig. 5a). You will be knotting ends "A" and "D" over cords "B" and "C" (or cord "BC"). Pass end "A" *over* cords "B" and "C" and under cord "D." Next, pass end "D" *under* cords "B" and "C" and over cord "A," bringing end "D" up through the loop formed between cord "B" and cord "A" (Fig. 5b). To complete the square knot, pass end "A" again *over* cords "B" and "C" and under cord "D"; then pass end "D" once again *under* cords "B" and "C," and bring out over the loop in cord "A" (Figs. 5c and 5d). Draw the knot tight.

Be sure to draw up your knots slowly and evenly when tightening them to ensure that each knot keeps its proper shape and balance.

When you have mastered the basic form of these 3 knots, cut 6 lengths of cord 4 or 5 yards long and do a sample piece based on the knotting pattern you will use in making the hammock. Concentrate on uniform, evenly tightened knots and on keeping the size of the open spaces the same.

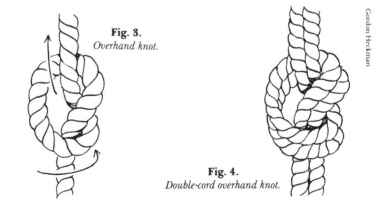

Fig. 3.
Overhand knot.

Fig. 4.
Double-cord overhand knot.

SAMPLE KNOTTING PATTERN

Fold each cord in half and pin the middles to the top of a board in a row. The board can be any substance that is flat and will hold pins — fiberboard or ceiling tile is good, as is a double-layer of corrugated cardboard, corrugated sides meshed together and taped. Pinning the folded cords will give you 12 ends to work with. Separate these ends into 2 groups of 6. Now proceed to knot according to the directions in the italicized portion of Step 5. When you feel comfortable with the results of your sample pattern, you are ready to begin your hammock.

MATERIALS

Two 1x2-inch hardwood boards, 28 inches long, for the end pieces. Sand them smooth and finish as desired.

One 10-pound roll of no. 150 cotton welt cord.

Two solid brass rings, each 3 inches in diameter.

Rubber bands, white glue, small nails, and hammer.

PREPARATION

In the 2-inch side of the wooden end pieces, drill seven ⅝-inch holes on 4-inch centers, starting 2 inches from an end.

Cut the cord into these segments: seven 11-yard pieces, which will be used folded in half; twenty-four 8-yard pieces; and two 3-yard pieces. Secure the cut ends with a wrapping of Scotch or adhesive tape to prevent raveling.

Gordon Heckman

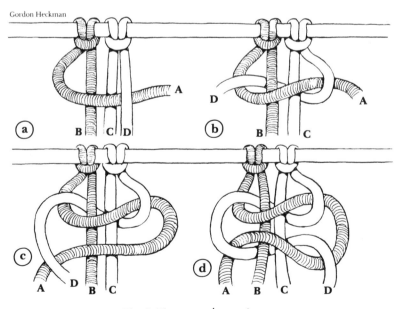

Fig. 5. *The macramé square knot.*

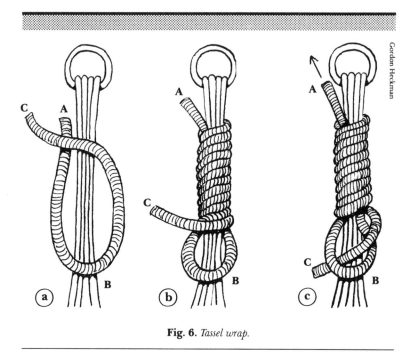

Fig. 6. *Tassel wrap.*

Because the finished length of the hammock is more than 10 feet, you will need quite a bit of space in which to work. The project should be hung against a surface to which it can be firmly attached with nails, because the knotting will have to be stretched out slightly while you are working on it. (A barn wall is ideal.) Also, you will need to move the knotting up as it gets longer and fasten it in place, making sure the rows are even and correctly spaced. In general, all knots should be pulled as tight as possible to reduce stretching. Measure frequently to be sure the pattern isn't getting out of scale. I use my tape measure a lot!

PROCEDURE

Basically, you will be starting at one end of the hammock, fastening the cords to one brass ring and then to an end piece. Once the cords are secured around the end piece, the body of the hammock is made from alternate rows of 2 knotting patterns, repeated until the desired length is reached. Then the second end piece is installed, and the second brass ring added to complete the hammock.

Step 1. Put the ends of the twenty-four 8-yard pieces, unfolded, through one of the rings. Fold over about 8 inches and secure the bundle with a very tight tassel wrap, using a 3-yard piece of cord to make the wrap. To make the tassel wrap, as shown in Fig. 6a, lay the short end "A" of the wrapping cord toward the ring. Carry the long end "C" toward the short ends of the cord bundle and make loop "B." Bring end "C" back up and wrap around whole bundle starting just below end "A."

Continue to wrap tightly down until only about 1 inch of loop "B" remains free (Fig. 6b). The total length of the wrapping should be 4 to 5 inches. Insert end "C" through loop "B" and pull end "A" until end "C" and loop "B" are both pulled inside the wrap (Fig. 6c). Trim wrapping cord ends. At the bottom of the wrap, trim the short ends of the hammock cords back to about an inch beyond wrap. Hang the work up by the ring against the knotting surface.

Step 2. Pull out 2 ends from each side of the bundle of cords. About 26 inches below the ring, tie an overhand knot (Fig. 3) in each pair. Make sure the knots are the same distance from the ring, as they will determine how level the wooden bar is. Take 1 end from each pair and pass it through the end hole in the bar, from the front, and pull the other end of the pair through from the back. Do this on both ends of the bar, pulling the bar up snug against the overhand knots and checking again to be sure it's level.

Step 3. Now take an 11-yard cord, folded in half. Hold the midpoint of the cord (the fold that marks the 5½-yard mark) behind an end hole, and triple-half-hitch (Fig. 2) each end to the bar on either side of the drilled hole. Tie 2 square knots (Fig. 5) in each group of 4 ends, pulling the knots tight and as close to the bar as possible. Repeat for the other end hole.

Step 4. From the remaining lengths hanging from the ring, take 4 cords from the center of the group and tie them in a square knot just above the bar at the center hole. Bring the middle 2 cords of the knot through the hole from front to back, and bring the outer 2 cords through from back to front. Tie a square knot just below the bar, using cords from the back as tying cords (Fig. 7). Repeat this for each hole, working from the center toward the ends. Check that the bar is level after each pair of holes is done.

Step 5. Next, take the rest of the folded 11-yard pieces and triple-half-hitch them to the bar, 1 to each hole (except for the ends, which you have already done). As with the end holes, the midpoint of the 11-yard cord should be held behind the hole, and the ends hitched 1 on each side of the hole. You will now have 6 ends below each hole (except for the end holes; with 4 ends each).

Separate each group of 6 into 2 groups of 3. Tie each of these 3's in a square knot, using a cord from the center square knot as a carrier line (the one that hangs down through the middle of the square knot). After these 2 square knots, tie the center 4 ends in another square knot. You should have a diamond shape made of 4 square knots (Fig. 7). Repeat this for each group of 6 ends. (For sample knotting pattern, with 12 ends only, the pattern is repeated only once, with the other 6 ends.)

Step 6. At this point, you might want to have a coffee break, or take a walk in your garden, or buy yourself a wonderful new garment suitable for hammock-swinging — anything to celebrate the fact that the worst is over and the rest of the hammock is child's play, relatively speaking.

Step 7. When you resume work, it's a big help to bundle and secure your working ends with rubber bands, so you don't have to pull so many yards of cord through each time (Fig. 8).

Step 8. Begin the next row under the wooden bar by taking 2 cords each from adjacent groups, starting at one end, and joining them with 2 square knots (see Figs. 7 and 8 for the pattern). The tops of the knots should be about 3½ or 4 inches below the edge of the bar. There will be 2 unused cords between each square knot in this row that should hang straight down.

Step 9. Repeat the first row under the wooden bar by bringing one cord from either side and square-knotting these onto the 2 idle cords hanging down. Be sure the diamond shape made by the cords is uniform (Fig. 8). Now bring another cord from each side and make two 3-cord square knots side by side; then repeat the center 4-cord square knot, as you did in Step 5. This should give you a diamond of square knots directly below the first row, with a 7-inch space between. The outer group of 4 cords will have 2 square knots, as in the first row. Try to make these outer knots right under the first row so that the knotting will not get narrower as the work progresses. These outer knots should be nailed to the wall as they are completed; also secure some of the other knots in each row.

Step 10. Alternate Steps 8 and 9, keeping the rows level, until the knotting extends about 7 feet. The second wooden bar should be added after a row of square-knot diamonds (Step 9). Hold the bar under the row, and pull the center 2 cords of each group of 6 through the hole below it from front to back. Then take the cords on either side of the center and bring them through the hole from back to front. Tie a square knot directly below the bar with these 4 ends (as you did in Step 2). This end should be a mirror image of the top. Make sure the second end piece or bar is *parallel* to the first. For the end holes, just put the center 2 cords through the hole, one from each side, and tie them in an overhand knot. For the time being, ignore the 2 outer cords from each group of 6 that you haven't yet used.

Step 11. Get the other brass ring, the 3-yard tassel-wrap cord, and a heavy rubber band. Gather all the hammock-cord ends (except the ones you're ignoring) in one hand and try to form a smooth, even group with a minimum of twisting, sagging, or criss-crossing of cords. Center the ring below the bar at a distance equal to that between the top ring and bar. Pass the ends of the cords through the ring from front to back, fold them over, and secure them with the rubber band. Check that the ring is centered and the cords are uniformly tight, and adjust as necessary. At this point, you could unnail the hammock and turn it upside down to check uniformity of the tension before doing the tassel wrap.

Fig. 7.
*Detail illustrating
Steps 4 and 5.*

Fig. 8.
*Steps 8 and 9 alternate to
produce a diamond pattern.
Ends are bundled to prevent
tangling.*

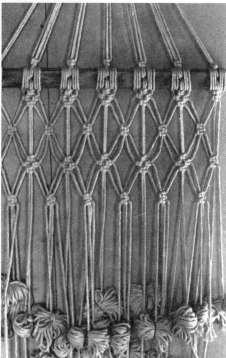

Ira Gavrin and Sidne Lewis

Remove the rubber band and make a tight tassel wrap, starting close to the ring (see Step 1). Trim the loose ends below the wrap.

Step 12. Hang the hammock by the ring you just added. Triple-half-hitch the ends you had been ignoring to the bar next to the holes, as in Step 3. Bring each pair of ends to the back of the bar and tie them together in a square knot soaked in white glue. Once the glue dries, cut the ends off close to the knot. You are now the proud possessor of one beautiful, handmade hammock. Because it is cotton and subject to discoloring and rotting if left outside for too long, bring it inside on rainy days. (But because it is cotton, it is soft and comfortable next to your skin.)

Step 13. Hang your hammock between 2 trees so that it is stretched out almost straight. Fix yourself a glass of lemonade and climb aboard.

SOURCES

Cotton welt cord can be hard to find these days, but can be ordered from: Seattle Marine, 2121 West Commodore Way, Seattle, WA 98199. Other types of cordage can, of course, be used, but cotton is by far the most comfortable for the purpose and the easiest to work with.